Par Sands and th

Par Sands lies on the south coast of Cornwall between the port of Fowey to the east and Mevagissey to the west.

The name Par means swamp or sand or a bar of mud and sand. In 1644 it was known as Le Pare and up to the early years of the 19th century the village comprised just a few houses situated at the foot of a cliff overlooking the estuary of the Par river, an expanse of water that could be crossed via a ferry. After these years the area started to grow, as did industry via the development of the assets of copper, granite and china clay which could all be found in the locality.

The growth was also due to the activities of Joseph Austen from Fowey. Born in 1782, the businessman was later to change his name to Joseph Treffry. His interests included pits, as well as mines such as a copper mine at Lanescot, an asset destined to grow and become the Fowey Consols mine. One of his ideas was to connect such workings with the docks at Fowey via a tramway, but when that became impossible because he couldn't purchase the land required, he decided to turn his attention towards developing a harbour at Par instead. Up until then ships were pulled up on Par beach to load or unload, an action leading to some of them being wrecked.

In response, Treffry's initial move was to build a bridge in 1824 as a replacement for the ferry, which he had bought, before moving on to creating the harbour itself. A canal and tramways were then formed to allow the transportation of copper ore from the mine to the harbour and were in use until the mining of copper started to fall away and the china clay industry emerged, and grew.

The port of Fowey always continued to be important, however, despite the rise of Par with its 450' breakwater. This was because, due to the tides, the depth of water at Par was only ever 16 feet, meaning that large ocean-going ships could not be accommodated there.

Par harbour and the beach at Par lie south of the village while the smaller beach of Spit lies west of the harbour. Par has a wide, shallow, sandy beach with expanding dunes, backing on to a local nature reserve that includes the Par beach pond, the feature of this 'year round' view of life on the lake. A brackish pond, it is half sea water and half river water, featuring reeds that benefit from such conditions.

The pool is abundant with fish, and attracts a wide range of bird life. Once a model boating lake, it is connected to the sea via a sluice gate and a channel. It has been in place for over a century.

Walkers on the South West Coast Path can view the area as the lake can be seen from the Path, which includes Par Beach in its route, and also briefly coincides with the Saints' Way there.

Overlooking both the beach, and the lake, are the houses of East Polmear, the word Polmear meaning Big Pool or Great Pool in Cornish. Par beach itself was sold by Arthur Francis Bassett of Tehidy to Tywardreath Parish Council from the high water mark of ordinary tides to the Par to Fowey Great Western Railway line in 1914, the purchase price being £100. The Par to Fowey railway no longer exists, but the Haul Road has taken its place, this a private road for china clay traffic between Fowey and Par Docks.

Par Beach

and residents

A YEAR IN THE LIFE OF A CORNISH LAKE

January 1

The first day of a New Year settles over the lake which laps between the old cliffs of Par and the sand-dunes, with the grey Atlantic stretching and rolling beyond. Par was once a tiny harbour, used by a few fishing boats, but mineral wealth led to its expansion. It became a port for the copper trade, the docks implemented in 1829 by Joseph Treffry, but later was to be a main port for the export of china clay - until that recently settled into slow decline. The lake, now a recognized nature reserve, also evolved over the years as Par beach and docks did.

January 2

Seagulls shelter in swathes along the lake's edge, making any available perch their own. Among them are Black-headed gulls (*Larus ridibundus*), who have lost their dark, chocolate-brown, hoods due to their winter plumage. Numbers of Black-headed gulls have expanded over the last 70 years, many favouring coastal sandhills and shingle banks for nesting. Nesting is in the future. At the moment, at Par, they await the next visitor to the lake, bearing corn for them to devour.

January 3

The affable, gregarious and striking Canada geese (*Branta Canadensis*) have adopted the lake with relish over the past three years. At one time their appearance was a rarity. Now they are so much in residence there are days when their numbers seem to reach many hundreds. The goose was introduced to Britain as an ornamental bird from North America around 280 years ago. A crafty few found freedom, flying from the lakes of collectors, and they have led to a population explosion in Britain. They can frequently be seen in 'V' formations in the air.

January 4

There was a time when only one pair of determined mute swans ruled the pond. They bred annually, but chased their cygnets away when the time came for the youngsters to establish their own territory. However, now the lake is shared by a large number of pairs of such swans (*Cygnus olor*) – whose cygnets stay much longer than they were allowed to do in past years. Legend has it that the first pair of mute swans came to Britain via Richard the Lionheart who brought them back from Cyprus following the Third Crusade. Nevertheless, the prevailing thought is they were probably bred in the country long before this.

January 5

Before an increase in the number of swans, and the arrival – in their masses – of the Canada geese, the lake belonged mainly to the mallards (*Anas platyrhynchos*). Despite being outnumbered now they seem to mingle happily with the new-comers, competing with them for food from the lake, and from residents bearing gifts.
At this time of year, the drake has his glossy green head, white collar and purple-brown breast while the duck is drabber, and brown. But between July and September they take on 'eclipse plumage' when the drake is almost identical to the duck, but slightly darker.

January 6

Today a bone-numbingly cold spell of weather hit the area, leaving the lake frozen.
With Cornwall usually experiencing warm, wet winters the lake is rarely covered by ice to such an extent.
Bewildered gulls stand on the ice, confused by what has happened to their normal surroundings.

January 7

Ice continues to dominate in parts
of the lake, to the consternation
of one of the swans, who finds
that the water has changed its
appearance..
Overlooking the pool are the
cottages and houses of Polmear,
most of the 'newer' houses being
built in the 1930s.
Between the buildings and the lake
lie the cliffs where the sea used to
reach an area now serving as fields
and sand dunes.

January 8

The ice starts to melt in patches, giving
the swans the chance to groom
themselves again in the water.
Swans were controlled in Britain for
centuries by royal swanherds, or courts
called 'swanmotes'.
Those swans who were owned privately
were stopped from flying away by being
'pinioned'.
A mark of ownership could also be made
by branding them or make a swan mark
in the skin of the upper bill.

January 9

As a dying sun lends a touch of fire
to the reeds, a large percentage of
the lake's feathered population gather around a generous visitor who has
arrived with corn for them, as a sunset snack.
Knowingly, the swans and geese
stand nearest to their benefactor, to
keep out the foraging gulls.
Temperatures have improved and
the lake's surface is back to its fluid
normality.

January 10

A crowd of screaming gulls flock for food, determined to make the most of any scraps available.
If food is not to be found the black-headed gulls will turn to crabs, sand-eels, moths, snails, earthworms and insects instead.
The most determined tend to be the herring gulls, who will take eggs and chicks in the spring if the opportunity arises.

January 11

A dispute among some of the mute swans leads to flashes of angry white wings. Usually they are able to escape each other, but the cold snap has left them with less of the lake to be able to swim in. These swans are not exactly mute as they are able to snort and hiss when angered. Some can also produce a weak trumpeting.

January 12

Rain arrives, driving across the beach and pond, and the thaw is complete. Raindrops splatter the reeds, home of the heron, and the Cornish gorse which grows by the side of the lake and provides valuable cover for birds (especially their nests), rabbits and other wildlife.
The bright yellow, fragrant, flowers can usually be found blooming whatever time of the year for, as the saying goes:
'When gorse is out of blossom, kissing's out of fashion'.
The plant is also known as furze or whin.

January 13

Still wetter and slightly warmer. A Cayuga duck, with its eye-catching iridescent green plumage, swims along with a group of mallards, having either been left on the lake after being kept in captivity, or having escaped from captivity.
Cayugas descend from ducks kept on Cayuga Lake, one of the lakes in New York State.

January 14

Coots gather with mute swans, and ducks, by the reeds which offer a haven for water birds wanting to shelter from predators. Coots can show real aggression, and often deter enemies by kicking up spray in their faces. They paddle quickly into the reeds if a bird of prey is seen, raising spray as they dive to safety. However, their white flash on their forehead makes them easily recognizable, however grey the weather.

January 15

Clinging to the branches of trees overhanging the lake, pitted today by rainwater, are lichens. Those growing on plants, particularly on the trunks and branches of trees, are called epiphytes, epi meaning 'on the surface' and phyte meaning 'plant'. Every lichen is the result of two or more separate organisms living together – permanently. They first appeared 400 million years ago.

January 16

A pair of swans start investigating the reeds, perhaps planning ahead for nesting season.
Creatures of habit, swans often mate for life and breed in the same place each year, so they are 'exploring' very well known territory.
They build large, sturdy nests from sticks and vegetation at the water's edge.

January 17

Two mallards find shelter as morning develops.
The wind is rising and will almost reach gale force by evening, with thunder and lightning at night.
A darkening sky lowers as the reeds are whipped by the wind's force.

January 18

A day of mixed weather – hail, sun and rain. There seems to be something of the ancient Louisiana bayou about the area as the water levels rise still. A fungus hugs one of the trees.
Fungi contribute to nature's continuous rebirth, recycling dead organic matter into useful nutrients.
Many plants depend on fungi for their own nutrients.

January 19

Gusts of sleet, spatters of sun, scything winds—again the weather arrives in a variety of forms which have combined to heighten the water level.

A busy 'dot' mid-lake turns out to be a swimmer and gastronomic seabird extraordinaire, a cormorant. Cormorants can consume more than their own weight of fish in a day, which is something that this bird is happy to prove. Its diet includes wrasse, sand-eels and the occasional crab.

January 20

All fear of people has evaporated for the lake's swans and geese.

As soon as someone approaches them with anything that looks as if it might be food, or stops in a car, they are there, waiting and hoping.

One of the swans peers through a car window in anticipation of culinary delights following.

January 21

Driving rain continues unabated which means that levels keep on relentlessly rising.

The boggy floodplain which surrounds the lake, and which has developed where the river used to run in bygone years, is gorged with water. Indeed, the river at one time reached Par itself, a sloop having sunk at a place where a shop now stands.

January 22

With heavy rain overnight the stream running parallel to the entrance to the beach, and which is part of the system connecting with the lake, has risen visibly.

Daffodils are in bud and are now peeking well above the soil along the bank.

January 23

Jackdaws intermingle with the seagulls, ducks and geese. Jackdaws, once simply called 'daws', can be seen feeding amongst rooks or starlings in fields, and have been caught perching on horses or sheep to pluck out tufts of hair to line their nests.

Indeed, they will eat almost anything that comes their way, although animal food and grain seem to be preferred.

January 24

The edges of the lake are seeping slowly into surrounding grassland, expanding the area where the wild residents can seek shelter.

This area was once completely under water, the sea being able to creep its way up to St Blazey. Marshland to the south of St Blazey mainly resulted from years of streaming tin. It was in the 1820s that the whole appearance of Par began to alter, however, due to Joseph Treffry's desire to build a canal and construct a harbour.

January 25

Azure skies change the colour of the lake to a landscape more reflective of summer.
The lake, photographed from the sand-dunes, is peaceful.
Most Cornish dunes comprise wind-blown calcareous sand. Those at Par are gradually expanding across the beach.

January 26

Seagulls wheel at dusk above the lake.
The sky they are circling in is a wash of fading blues and greys, evidence of the mixed weather which dominated the day – rain and splashes of sun.

January 27

With continuous rain forming a sea of mud under the trees by the lake swans sift through the puddles for food, gathering together in a hunting party!
Mute swans can defend their territory very aggressively, and often there is only one pair per smaller lake.
However, when there is enough food to go round they can live happily enough in a colony.

January 28

The rain abates for a day to be replaced by blue sky and January sun. Canada geese line the edge of the lake looking on at the reeds which a setting sun gilds. Mallards have slipped into the reeds, one flying over them as the geese watch on. When they fly Canada geese do so in family groups, the parents carefully accompanying their youngsters.

January 29

Oystercatchers fly from the lake where they have sought food, helped in their quest by the sodden ground.
Conspicuous by their bold black and white plumage and long orange bills they look for worms and insects while on land, and for shellfish by the edge of the sea.
Once they find shellfish they rap them with their bills and then prise them open, evidence of their 'work' found near the lakeside.

January 30

Gulls huddle on the side of the lake as cold wind and rain whip across the water. Meanwhile swans hide amongst the vegetation along the waterway.
The rising land in the distance is swathed in curtains of rain, while the lake is ruffled by the strong northerly gusts.

The small flock of oystercatchers takes off from the side of the lake where the birds have been searching again for worms in the wet earth, prodding it with their orange bills.
Their warning 'kleep kleep' sound echoes across the water, which has continued to rise in the flood plain.

February 1

A solitary crow sits in a tree overlooking the lake, taking in the clear but cold weather. The carrion crow (*Corvidae*) is completely black and is usually seen alone, although is sometimes spotted in pairs. Clever and adaptable, it is a fearless bird.
At the same time, new born lambs follow their mother in the field above the nature reserve.
Snow is forecast and the temperature drops during the day.

February 2

A rare visitor to the lake – a Bar-Headed goose – joins in with the Canada geese.
The visitor, whose home is usually in Burma, stayed around for a few days and then continued its journey. This goose is one of the world's highest flying birds, migrating over the Himalayas to winter in India, Burma and Pakistan.
It is often bred in captivity and those spotted in Britain are usually escapees.

February 3

Snow blankets Cornwall and with the 'white stuff' comes ice, which covers the lake while the snow itself smothers the sand on the beach, and fields around.
Wildlife congregates on land, alongside the lake, searching for something to eat, and waiting for the melt.
Lambs make the most of the grass they can find in the fields above the bay once the thaw begins to set in.

Snow turns back to rain, and that and the melted slush make the grass around the lake wringing wet. Behind a gathering of swans coots bathe in the puddles on the grass, rather than in the lake itself. Coots are all black, apart from their distinctive white beak with a 'shield' above, and are larger than their cousins, the moorhens. There are lobed flaps of skin on their toes to aid their swimming.

February 5

There are clearer skies, resplendent with a few blue patches, although snow has been reported as falling in some depth in the Bristol area. A heron perches in a tree near the island, watching for food. The heron has a pick-axe bill used to catch its fish which, if small, are swallowed whole. If larger they are stabbed repeatedly before expertly having the flesh taken from their bones on the lakeside edge.

February 6

More flurries of snow arrive in the county, although mainly blanketing the north coast.
Despite the south staying snow-free, a freezing wind hits the lake, leaving the swans to huddle at the far end, out of the worst of the icy blasts.
The water becomes choppy, dancing with mini-waves, while on the seashore turnstones choose to search for food by the more sheltered River Par, rather than on the shoreline.

February 7

The catkins are out, braving a bitter wind which ruffles the surface of the pond, making distinctive waves.

Catkins appear before the leaves so they can be pollinated by the wind. If the leaves were on the tree first, the pollen might stick to them.

Male catkins begin to develop in autumn. They are long and brownish/yellow in colour. Early the following spring they become a creamy/yellow. Female catkins are small and brown with bright red styles, ripening after the male catkins.

February 8

The temperature still hasn't risen, and the rain returns with a force which will not be denied. Black-headed gulls dance on the damp grass to entice the worms!! Although this pair are hunting for food quite peacefully together their species can be quarrelsome and very noisy.

February 9

The rain remains, falling in bucketfuls. Strong winds and the heavy, prolonged showers have created huge puddles which seep through the grass.

Swans, perhaps seeking shelter from the weather, have made their way up the small, sheltered, stream and are sieving the puddles by the roadside.

February 10

Three mallards—a duck and two drakes—explore the flooded undergrowth in search of food. A stillness has crept over the weather, but so far has resulted in no drop in the water level.
Mallards breed in the UK in both summer and winter, wherever there are suitable wetland habitats. Those in this country could be resident, but some of the birds that breed in Iceland and other parts of Northern Europe spend their winter here.

February 11

Blue skies dominate and nature hints, at last, that spring might be only a month or two away.
But the man-made signs in the lake demonstrate how the water has risen throughout the past wet weeks.
Two Canada geese swim past the 'deep water' sign which now has the words 'no swimming' obscured by the level of the lake.
It's not a notice they pay any attention to anyway.

February 12

In the trees by the side of the reeds a chaffinch surveys the area as dusk starts to fall.
One of the most abundant birds in the UK, the chaffinch has a variety of songs and calls and recognisable plumage.
The plumage is even more evident in flight, when it reveals a flash of white on the bird's wings, and on its tail feathers.

February 13

A still morning, with warmer temperatures—time for the Canada geese to have a wash and a brush up.

Canada geese, like these, usually migrate northwards after breeding, with those who have lost nests early in the breeding season flying anywhere from several to more than 1500 kilometres.

After their journey, they tuck into vegetation in an earlier state of growth to fuel their moult.

February 14

The rain and snow have abated for a few days and thoughts are straying to nesting. More swans than usual are exploring the reeds, where their nests are usually hidden from public view.

Their nests are large, being about four to five feet across, with shallow depressions in the middle. They tend to nest in secluded areas on shores, or in shallow water.

February 15

New buds are visible on the trees, proving that the grip of winter may be passing.

This feeling is compounded when skylarks can be heard in the sand dunes.

A rather drab, brown bird which is often inconspicuous when on the ground, this dullness is completely overcome by the skylark's distinctive, trilling song when it is rising high in the sky.

February 16

A pair of ducks start nesting, on their own in the water-logged undergrowth.
Although quite near where the public walk the overhanging trees help camouflage them.
Mallards will always choose to nest near water, if possible, choosing a place which is covered by vegetation. They like to have plentiful food near-by, as well, but often select a site which is not quite perfect.

February 17

Whitefront and a companion find a quiet space on their own by the side of the lake, near the blackthorn bushes in which the rabbits make their waterside home. New green shoots, other signs of approaching spring, peek above the lake's surface while the gorse continues to bloom.

February 18

A flotilla of swans swims determinedly towards someone bearing food. A fine day has brought out a number of visitors to the beach.
The mute swan breeds across most of the UK, although not on the moors of south-west England, in northern Scotland or in mid-Wales. Impressively they can fly at speeds of up to 55mph.

February 19

Another dry, fine morning greets the lake's inhabitants. Geese happily graze on the grass between the lake's edge and the road.
There are at least 11 sub-species of Canada goose. On the whole, the goose becomes smaller the more northwards you are, and the darker the more westwards you are.

February 20

With the sun out, and radiating warmth, more than it has done for some while, the swans just sit in its benevolent rays, and let the world go by.
The phrase 'swan song' comes from the belief of Aristotle, Socrates and Plato, that the swans' ability to sing becomes greater as death approaches.

February 21

A sense of peace enfolds the lake, its inhabitants continuing to enjoy the spell of fine, dry weather.
The winter sun shines not only upon the water but also—in the distance– on the walls of the manor of Trenython, peeping as always from between a stand of woodland high above Par.
Originally, it was built as a home for Colonel Peard as a gift after he supported Garibaldi during his campaign in Italy.

February 22

With the fine weather continuing an oyster catcher, often seen by the lake, seeking food on the grass after rain, perches instead on a rock by the harbour entrance.
Also spotted today are a squirrel, emerging from hibernation, and a shy water rail. The water rail or European water rail (*Rallus aquaticus*) is a small wetland bird. Its breeding habitats include marshes and reed beds across Europe.

February 23

Juvenile gulls take over their own space by the lakeside, their brown and white spotted plumage determining that they were last year's chicks, but have yet to reach adulthood. On some the grey feathers, and black tail feathers are just beginning to show through. There are squabbles galore between them when anyone arrives bearing food!
This familiar gull can be distinguished from other gulls by its large size and grey upperparts, which earn it the alternative names of 'silver back' and 'silvery gull'.

February 24

The daffodils are now starting to bloom, yellow showing from the green buds which had been tightly shut when the snow was on the ground.
Overall, the daffodils in Cornwall are slightly later in blooming this year.
The earliest known reference to daffodils can be found in the 6th century AD writings of Prophet Mohammed.

February 25

Sited on its own, by the reeds, is a Shoveler duck. Surface feeding ducks, they have large spatulate bills. The males have dark green heads, with white breasts and chestnut flanks while the females are mottled brown.

In flight the birds show patches of light blue and green on their wings. They breed in southern and eastern England and, in smaller numbers, in Scotland and western parts of England.

February 26

Hiding away on his, or own, is a white duck who has happily made the lake its winter home.

The day has been quiet and peaceful, especially now as dusk has started to creep in, gradually shrouding the lake in settling darkness.

February 27

Fighting has broken out among some of the many swans, with one bearing down and two with wings raised, ready for battle. Mute swans are not constantly quiet. They can snort when annoyed., and trumpet when really angry.

Territorial birds, they will indulge in vicious fighting if they feel their territory is threatened by an intruder.

This time the mallard drakes start squabbling, probably over a woman – as the females are now in much demand. Some of the pairs have disappeared from the main lake, and are upstream, building nests or tending to a clutch of eggs.

March 1

A beautiful day, with a warmth which falsely makes you believe that winter is at an end.
From his perch in a tree a wood pigeon surveys a view which will take in the lake, and the Atlantic waves.
The UK's largest and commonest pigeon, the wood pigeon is largely grey with a white neck patch and white wing patches, clearly visible in flight.

March 2

A quiet, reflective start to the evening. The swans are less determined to 'mug' the visitor for food, just inquisitive.
Their diet is mainly aquatic vegetation and roots with a little dash of aquatic insects added in. Small fish and tadpoles won't be turned down either!
They put their long necks underwater to tug at the aquatic plants, rather than diving.

March 3

The rain pours down with a vengeance once again, turning the lakeside muddy, as well as making the streams running into it a turgid brown colour.
The grass is awash and the waterways that flow into the pool have risen to a height that will cause them to flood their surrounding areas.

March 4

A mixed bag of a day following a cold night.
The lake's community saw rain, sleet and sun. By afternoon the sun dominated so one of the Canada geese decided just to relax in its rays.
Geese often mate for life, and can pine to death when they lose their mate.
Devoted parents, they never leave their goslings unguarded.

March 5

Blackbirds are part of the family of chats and thrushes known as *Turdidae*.
Although the males are strikingly black the females are duller, being brown and often having spots and streaks on their breast.
The male also sports a bright orange –yellow beak and eye-ring.

March 6

A Ring-necked dove watches on from the trees, while his mate hides in the ivy, out of sight. These doves are usually found alone or in pairs, although they do form larger flocks around sources of food and water, these sometimes containing hundreds of birds.

The doves are quite noisy in these groups, not only for the variety of calls they make throughout the day, and often throughout the night, but also because their wings clap loudly when the birds take flight.

March 7

Flowers are now starting to flourish. Snowdrops - *Galanthus*—have been out for a while and now daisies are showing through with the rabbits out feasting on the new leaves.

Galanthus nivalis is the best known and most widespread representative of the genus. It is native to a large area of Europe.

Although it is often thought of as a British native wild flower, or to have been brought to the British Isles by the Romans, it was probably introduced around the 16th century.

March 8

A sharp wind whips across the lake, stirring up waves, making the surface slightly resemble the sea which is pounding away over the other side of the dunes.

On the pool, however, there are wavelets but none of the 'white horses' which are evident in Par Bay. The wavelets do not deter the geese who power through the choppy water, despite many of the other residents choosing to take cover in the reeds.

March 9

The pied wagtails are out, pecking away in the grass, searching for food. A flock of them live in the trees around the lake.

In summer the male has a white forehead, cheeks and belly with a jet-black crown, nape, throat, breast, back, flanks, tail and wings. The tail has white outer feathers while the wing bars have white on them too.

In winter, though, the non-breeding male has a greyer plumage with less black on the breast and a grey flank.

March 10

The cormorant returns on a day which sees enough sunshine to tempt people outside to feel the rays for a while. They are birds of the coast rather than the ocean, and some are found in inland waters. It is thought that the ancestor of cormorants could well have been a bird which frequented fresh water lakes.

March 11

Frogs will generally mate in the spring, depending on the weather, with the female laying eggs which the male will then fertilise. It is estimated that the average female frog can lay up to 4,000 eggs at one go although many of these eggs will not survive to turn into frogs.

One frog is discovered by eggs laid in a drain cover near the lake.

There seem to be more drakes than ducks among the mallards, the ratio of three to one, as seen here, being the average.
Two of the drakes sport white fronts, one a big, bright one, the other less so. There is a folk lore, especially in Scotland, that the colour of the wishbone of a male mallard, helps foretell the weather.
If their wishbones turn dark then harsh temperatures are ahead, whilst a pale wishbone indicates mild weather on its way.

March 12

The swans that have paired up are absent from view much of the day now – this duo hidden in the reeds and obviously planning for a future brood!
Swans begin to breed between three and four years of age.
They have the longest neck of any bird, with a total of 23-25 neck vertebrae.
They also have as many as 25,000 feathers.

March 13

A beautiful morning, with warm weather promised for the week ahead. Four swans are trying out their ablutions, and perhaps their mating rituals.
Swan mates display in a ritual which involves touching bill-to-bill and breast-to-breast, often forming a perfect heart shape, or entwining necks.

March 14

The blossom is starting to show, the evenings are drawing out, the mornings are lighter and spring is most definitely in the air. Wild flowers are used to show the spread of spring, the dates they appear being constantly monitored. For instance, primroses usually flower a month earlier in Cornwall than in the Cairngorms. Using the average of dates when wild flowers bloom has shown that spring advances at about two miles an hour across Britain.

March 15

It's been a sunny Sunday and two Canada geese who have been well fed settle down for a peaceful evening.

During the second year of their lives, Canada Geese find a mate.

They are monogamous, and most couples stay together all of their lives. If one is killed, the other may find a new mate. The female lays 4–8 eggs and both parents protect the nest while the eggs incubate.

March 16

Again, it has been warm throughout the day. One swan looks across a still lake during the late afternoon.

In eras gone by as well as being a source of food other parts of the swans were used; feathers as quills for writing; the leathery web for making purses and wing bones for making whistles.

It is possible that being a 'Royal bird' meant that such domestication saved the swan from becoming extinct in Britain.

March 17

Spring sunshine streams through the trees while the geese preen themselves by the side of the lake.

This week bird-watchers in St Austell Bay have reported a Manx Shear-water at nearby Gorran Haven, as well as a yellow-legged gull and a Common Scoter, a Marsh Harrier and a Goosander. The spring migrants have obviously started to arrive.

March 18

This time it is the turn of the Canada geese to make their way into the reeds to seek an ideal place to nest.
The geese seek their own territory in order to prevent the female being disturbed during egg laying and subsequent incubation. Their wish is to keep other geese and predators, including wild animals and humans, as far away as possible.

March 19

The sun shines down on the lake from the cliff walk where only a month or so before there was snow.
The coast path leads from Par around to Polkerris and then the port of Fowey, from where it meanders around the Fowey estuary.
Between Polkerris and Fowey lies Polridmouth. This area is linked with the author Daphne du Maurier who lived at nearby Menabilly.

March 20

The chaffinch (*Fringilla coelebs*), the commonest finch in the UK, is once again singing against a turquoise sky.
By the side of the lake this Par chaffinch sings in a tree which is showing new green, spring, buds and leaves.

March 21

Peeping amongst the grass are sweet violets (*Viola odorata*), flowers of the woodland margins and shady hedge banks.
The fragrance of its flowers is strong, and as a result it has been used in making perfumes from as long ago as Ancient Greece. It is apparently a myth that you can only smell the flowers once, but the strength of its scent fades.

March 22

There was a time when much of the area which the village of Par now covers was under water, due to the meeting of the mouths of two rivers—the Tywardreath River and St Blazey River.
Ferries would take passengers between St Blazey and Tywardreath, this form of transport probably falling by the wayside about 400 years ago as it was about then that the Tywardreath River began to disappear due to silt.
Much later on silting would extend to the St Blazey River.

March 23

Swans feature in Greek mythology in which the story of Leda and the Swan explains that Helen of Troy was conceived following the union of the Queen of Sparta Leda, and Zeus, when he was disguised as a swan.
One story which forms part of Norse mythology mentions a pair of swans that drink from the sacred Well of Urd in the realm of Asgard, which was home of the gods.
Apparently the well's water was so pure and holy all things that touched it turn white, including the original pair of swans and all others descended from them.

March 24

Among the first wild flowers spotted in the banks and hedgerows near the lake is the Red Campion (*Silene dioica*).
The genus *Silene* was named after *Silenus*, who was the merry god of the woodlands in Greek mythology.
This plant is dioecious which is to say that it bears its male and female flowers on separate plants, the male flowers being smaller than those on the female plant.

March 25

It may only be March, but there are signs that the May blossom will soon be out. The blossom is from the hawthorn tree which, according to legend, comprised the original Crown of Thorns. It is also believed to be bad luck to cut down a hawthorn.
Hawthorns can live for up to four centuries, most of them having been planted in the 18th century when they were used to divide wild pastures and common land into small enclosures for animals.
They can tolerate sea winds and salt, which is fortunate in this case, as the waves pound so near to where the hedge is sited.

March 26

The drakes start lining up to follow the ducks, hoping that they won't be left out when it comes to mating time. They only form pairs until the females lay their eggs. After that they are left by the males.

Around eight to 13 eggs are laid in the clutch which usually hatch after around 27-28 days of incubation. Fledging takes place in around 50-60 days.

The ducklings can feed and swim as soon as they hatch, their diet being insects. They stay close to their mothers for protection, though.

March 26 again

The cherry blossom, said to be an emblem of love and affection and an omen of good fortune, is flowering in all its glory.

In Japan the Meteorological Agency, and the Japanese public make notes of where and when the cherry blossom blooms throughout the country.

It moves northward as warmer weather moves northwards. There are even festivals, named Hanami, arranged at which the Japanese stand and admire the beauty of the blossom.

The fact that the blossom is so short-lasting seems to add to its attraction.

March 27

A pair of swans start their almost choreographed display which will lead to mating.

The average size of a clutch of eggs for a mute swan is between four and seven, with the incubation period being between 34-45 days.

Swans are the largest species in the family of ducks (*Anatidae*). They are unusual in that the males help with the incubation of the eggs, although this does also occur with whistling ducks.

March 28

In the foreground, whilst the majority of the lake's occupants rush for food supplied by visitors, two oystercatchers find food on their own.

Oystercatchers' diet varies according to their location. Those occurring inland concentrate on worms and insect larvae whilst those in estuaries eat bivalves and worms.

Their bills are long, blunt, and flattened, efficient for catching and opening oysters, mussels, and clams.

March 29

New reeds start to show through the beds around the far edge of the lake, adding to the fresh green of spring plants.

The common reed aids wildlife by providing cover for a number of birds such as the reed warbler and the great bittern.

Later in the year a bittern is spotted flying from the reeds, a brown 'heron' soaring across the lake.

March 30

Signs of summer appear as house martins are spotted swooping across the surface of the water. The small bird with glossy blue-black upper parts and pure white under-parts, with its forked tail, is very distinctive.

A member of the swallow family it spends much of its time on the wing, collecting insects.

Their winters are spent in Africa. Generally they appear in the UK from April onwards, returning to Africa around September.

March 31

Two mute swans fly with their necks extended and with regular slow wing beats.

Though they fly well, their takeoff requires a stretch of water tens of metres in length over which they 'run' and flap to gain speed. Swans rarely land where there is an insufficient runway for take-off.

As with wild swans, flying overhead, their approach was heralded by the whistle of their wings.

April 1

A pair of mute swans again display the classic 'heart' shape pose to show their affection for each other.

The swan is often seen as a masculine symbol, its pure white colour connected to the sun, which is also almost always a masculine deity.

The swan was linked in ancient Greece to the god of the Sun, Apollo.

Time will tell how many mating swans on the lake will produce cygnets as a result of their love matches.

April 2

Rabbits are frequently spotted by the side of the lake, many of them choosing to make their burrows in the nearby gorse and blackthorn bushes. The rabbit's long ears, which can be more than 10 cm (4 in) long, are probably adapted to detect predators. They have large, powerful hind legs. Each foot has five toes, with one greatly reduced in size. They are digitigrade animals which means they move around on the tips of their toes.

Rabbits are small mammals in the family *Leporidae*.

April 3

Deep in the reeds hides a shy reed warbler (*Acrocephalus scirpaceus*). A summer visitor to the UK the reed warbler is difficult to see as it is a plain bird, brown above and buff coloured underneath.
In winter the birds can be spied in Africa, but while in the UK they choose to live in reed beds, their singing often giving away their presence.

April 4

An oyster catcher searches for food near the edge of the lake. Its Latin name is *Haematopus ostralegus* whilst its nickname is 'sea pie'.
Most UK birds spend the winter by the sea, where they are joined in the east by birds from Norway.
Because it eats cockles, the population can struggle if cockle beds are overexploited.
Watching on is an adult herring gull with a light grey back, white back, white under parts, and black wing tips with white 'mirrors'.

April 5

A little carpet of common violets peeps through emerald grass.
Common violets are from two to eight inches tall, with the flowers shyly evident within heart shaped leaves, which may be 3 to 5 inches wide.
Flowers are deep blue to violet with a lighter centre.
They are found in moist woods, fields, by roadsides and on lawns.
This plant has been used as a symbol of love and faithfulness.

April 6

The Song thrush—*Turdus philomelos*—seen searching for worms by the path near the pool, is from the family of chats and thrushes.
Its numbers are seriously declining, especially on farmland. It is smaller and browner than a Mistle thrush and its habit of repeating song phrases distinguishes it from a blackbird.
The Song thrush feeds on snails, which it breaks into by smashing them against a stone, used as an anvil, with a flick of the head.

April 7

Growing by the Par river is thrift, otherwise known as the Sea pink.
A perennial plant, it carpets cliffs and salt marshes from April through to July.
As its alternative name states, it has pink flowers which are set within deep green leaves that resemble grass.
It featured on the old three-penny bit and is an excellent plant for butterflies and moths seeking nectar.

April 8

Sun glistens on the surface of the lake, which has been mainly left, this morning, to the mute swans.
For many centuries they were kept for food in England, but face perils from different avenues these days. Due to ingesting a large amount of grit which is required to help them digest their food they often swallow lead that has been abandoned by fishermen.
After breaking down in their system this then damages nerves and muscles.

April 9

Mute Swans are family-orientated, and those at Par seem — most of the time—to be one big family.
They nest on large mounds that they build in shallow water in the middle or at the edge of a lake.
These monogamous birds re-use the same nest each year, restoring or rebuilding it as needed.
Male and female swans share the care of the nest, and once the cygnets are fledged it is not uncommon to see whole families looking for food.

April 10

The mallards are currently in their impressive courtship, with this pair of males preening themselves to ensure that they look their best.
However, after the drakes leave their mates to the job of raising the young, they fly to a secluded area and undergo their annual moult. The moulting of their wing feathers leaves them temporarily flightless. They are no longer displaying their courtship plumage, but a drab "eclipse" plumage is similar to that of a female.

April 11

A newly-arrived swallow sits high on an electricity wire not far from the lake.
The body shape of swallows is streamlined and slender with long-pointed wings which helps them hunt insects on the wing.
Their flight is very efficient allowing them to forage at around 40 mph, although they are capable of reaching speeds of between 65 mph when travelling.

April 11 again

A lamb huddles close to its mother in the fields above the lake. Most lambs will begin standing within an hour of birth. In normal situations, lambs nurse after standing, receiving vital milk.

Horses can also be seen in the fields near them, and today the animals are benefiting from fine weather and fresh grass.

The sheep are grazing on the fields to the east of the lake, these sited above the cliffs that wind their way around the coast eastwards until the River Tamar is eventually reached.

April 12

Another fine day with a blue, cloudless sky, the blue reflected on the sea and on the lake which is sited in front of Par beach.

Both beach, and lake, can be viewed from the coastal walk from Par which will take the hiker up to Gribbin Head to the east where the 26 metre tall Gribbin Daymark is sited. This was erected by Trinity House and has been in place since 1832. Its intention is to ensure sailors did not mistake the shallow water around Fowey for the deeper waters at the entrance to Falmouth.

April 13

The grass at the side of the lake is green at this moment, but later in the year, as the warmer and drier weather arrives, the grass tends to disappear.

At this time it is then gradually replaced by dusty, sandy soil, which leaves geese and swans flying elsewhere, now and then, to find food.

April 14

A Ring-necked dove (*Streptopelia capicola*) hides in one of the trees leading up to the lake. Other names for this species are the Cape turtle dove and the Half-collared dove. Ring-necked doves rest in treetops during the night and forage for food on the ground, drinking mainly in the morning.

April 15

Happy in each other's company, two black-headed gulls (*Larus ridibundus*) share a perch and gaze over the lake.

Despite its name these birds have a white head for most of the year. They are extremely common and enjoy gathering in flocks. They also like making a lot of noise as they join together in a quarrelsome cloud—especially when food is around and when they are roosting.

April 16

A brood of mallard ducklings sit together, contemplating the lake. Ducklings such as these are able to feed themselves as soon as they reach the water, although they have to work out what delicacy is edible. They need their mother, especially at night, to keep them warm when the weather is chilly. The cold can be deadly for them because their down is not naturally weatherproof.

April 17

When they start nesting especially, mute swans can become extremely territorial. This pair have retreated into the reeds to build their nest, avoiding the close proximity of other such pairs.

It has been observed that closeness of nests can lead to problems, with some newly hatched cygnets becoming attached to the wrong parent birds.

April 18

Ducklings gather for safety in the shallows, underneath the gorse bushes which shade the side of the lake. A male mallard keeps guard whilst, not far away, a heron fishes for a meal. The mother duck initially leads the ducklings to water, no matter how far away this might be, the advice being not to interfere to avoid her panicking and abandoning her charges.

April 19

Common bluebells (*Hyacinthoides non-scripta*) start to show their familiar lavender flowers, giving thoughts to rambling through extensive bluebell woods.

Other names for this much-loved wild flower include auld man's bell; calverkeys; jacinth; ring-o'-bells; and wood bells.

It is thought that when large numbers of bluebells carpet the countryside they indicate the presence of ancient woodland.

A mother mallard keeps a close watch on her brood as they start to become part of the lake's other inhabitants, these including species such as the Canada geese.

The wild mallard and the Muscovy duck (*Cairina moschata*) are thought to be the ancestors of all domestic ducks

These ducklings, although starting on their path to independence, will need their mother for a while yet, especially for safety when darkness falls.

April 21

On guard by the edge of the lake, waiting to pounce on any fish which dare swim along, is a little egret (*Egretta garzetta*), a member of the bittern and heron family.

The little egret has white plumes on his crest and black legs and bill, with yellow feet. A relatively new visitor to the UK, it first appeared in significant numbers around twenty years ago.

April 22

Wild flowers are beginning to paint the areas around the lake, with splashes of colour, such as pink and lavender, evident amongst the quickly growing, lush, spring grass.

Over the years flowers have also started spreading much further in the growing sand dunes between lake and beach.

April 23

Swathes of golden gorse begin to brighten the lakeside and the nearby sand dunes. This is a plant which grows best in poor conditions, and is often used for land reclamation, for example areas where mining has previously taken place. It helps wildlife by providing thorny cover for nesting birds, and rabbits. Rabbit burrows are especially evident under the gorse bushes near Par pool.

April 24

A grey heron stands motionless in the reeds, with its thick black stripe of feathers above its eye. In fully mature herons this stripe will then extend behind its head, growing out in a large tuft. Herons can eat frogs, insects, fish, even water voles and sometimes young water birds. A patient hunter, they will quietly watch the water for moving creatures, standing motionless, ready to strike as soon as they see dinner swim along.

April 25

Noisy herring gulls (*Larus argentatus*) draw attention to themselves, unaware that they are venturing on to the road which runs alongside the pool. They are large gulls which frequent coasts and rubbish tips as well as reservoirs and lakes. The adults have backs of light grey with white under parts and black wing tips, with 'mirrored' markings. Their feet are pink and webbed, whilst their bills are heavy and slightly hooked with a distinctive red spot.

The mute swan in the UK is generally a tame bird—and those at Par certainly are when visitors arrive in the car park, bearing seed for them. The birds often congregate near the car park, in anticipation.

The mute swan has long been domesticated in this country, where its history dates back centuries.

This, the most common swan, was also domesticated by the Greeks and Romans.

April 27

In the ten years up to 1990 around 250 little egrets were recorded in England, a definite rise on the 33 birds spied in the country in 1960.

They have mainly established themselves along the south coast—the initial sighting of this attractive member of the heron family thought to be in Poole harbour.

They then spread to areas such as Thorney Island and Cornish estuaries.

Little egrets have been breeding in England for around 25 years.

April 28

Ducklings forage on the grass alongside their mother. The drake may be absent as they tend to leave their mates around now to seek a secluded area to undergo their annual moult.

They find areas which supply a rich source of food, as moulting strips them of a great deal of energy.

For a while they will be unable to fly and they will take on a less striking plumage.

April 29

Unsettled, wet weather is marking the end of the month, with puddles developing by the lakeside as the ground becomes sodden.
There were gale force winds in the South West of England on April 25, with heavy rain washing across the county and localised flooding.
On this day the Met Office reported 44.5mm being recording in Perranporth. The rain failed to abate the following day and by today standing water is evident in many areas, with the level of the pool also rising.
During this spell of weather there have been thunderstorms and flash flooding in St Ives.

April 30

The mallard ducklings are growing in confidence and are definitely now part of the lake's inhabitants.
They usually have colouring with some yellow in it, clove-brown markings on their backs, a dark ear spot and a brown line through their eye area.
If predators threaten to strike, their mother will try to draw attention away from them, to herself, by quacking loudly and flapping her wings as if wounded.
The juvenile feathers begin to grow once the ducklings are in the water and feeding for themselves.

May 1

An adult Canada goose keeps watch while two goslings take to the water behind.
When protecting their goslings the parents can be seen violently to chase away any creatures they deem to get too close, from jackdaws to human beings—that is after giving a warning, hissing sound initially.
Adult geese can form creches, comprising groups of a number of goslings and a few adults to care for them. Goslings start to fledge when between six to nine weeks, and do not leave their parents until the spring, when they may migrate.

May 2

The first yellow flag irises (*Iris pseudacorus*) start to show through the reeds by the edges of the lake.
This is one of two native irises, easily recognised by its large bright yellow flowers.
Such flowers most frequently grow on the margins of lakes, ponds and watercourses.
Called by some the 'Queen of the Swamp' it originated in the British Isles and Europe, but gardeners transported it around the globe in the early 1900s.

May 3

Two herring gulls seem to be involved in gathering debris from the side of the pool for a nest.
The gulls are usually monogamous, and nest near the water in large colonies.
When courting, the male takes part in a series of moves which include tossing the head, feeding his partner, displays of 'choking' and calling to his lady friend.
Grass and moss are used to construct the nest which is lined with feathers and soft vegetation.

May 4

Gradually adding colour to the sand dunes are the scented flowers of the wild rose, *rosa rugosa*. In Japan and China, where this plant has been cultivated for about a thousand years, the flowers are used to make pot pourri.
A fast growing, bushy rose, it loves sandy soil, and produces single, large flowers from May through to September.
It also produces a large hip— the biggest of any wild rose.
The leaves form a shiny, dark green cover across the dunes, ideal for wildlife to hide in.

May 5 and 6

There is evidence of new, or coming, life everywhere. This mallard is taking her four little ones for a swim near the edge of the lake, where it is safer.
The pair of swans, however, are looking after their cygnets on the kerbside to the entrance road to Par beach and its surroundings.

The need to be near water is uppermost in the minds of Canada geese when nesting, so Par's reed bed is an excellent place for them . Their nest is bowl shaped and lined with goose down, leaves and grass. They start nesting at about three years of age, and mate for life.

May 8

A female mallard protects her two surviving ducklings. This has been a stressful time for her altogether, for during the laying period such ducks lay more than half their body weight in eggs in a few weeks. Afterwards, she needs a great deal of rest, depending on the male to protect her as she does recuperate.

May 9

The cow parsley (*Anthriscus sylvestris*) is in blossom near the lake, its white lacy flowers brightening grassy verges. Other names it is known by range from whiteweed to fairy lace and keck to Queen Anne's lace. The latter name is said to stem from the lace pillows Queen Anne carried while travelling the countryside. They were said to resemble the flowers. A member of the carrot family, it grows to about 5' high and flowers from April to August.

May 10

Although mainly a city bird the House sparrow (*Passer domesticus)* can certainly be found in this Cornish village setting.

Perching on the telephone wires this sparrow has an aerial view of the lake, around which it feeds on seeds, buds and the green parts of plants, together with insects in the summer.

During the spring and summer a pair of House sparrows can raise as many as four broods, the young fledging within 17 days.

The nest itself can be hidden in a crevice, a tree or even behind a drainpipe.

May 11

Alone in its own world a Common sandpiper (*Tringa hypoleucos*) searches for worms, insects, spiders or larvae beside the lake. Unusually, it is the male who cares most for the young birds when they hatch. He mainly incubates the eggs and later leads them to food and provides protection for them. The mother, on the other hand, shows little maternal dedication and only stays around for a few days.

May 12

The new goslings are growing fast and becoming accustomed to life on the pool. They are confident in the protection offered by the adults, following them as they swim between the lakeside and the reeds.

When the young are grown the families will join together to fly around the surrounding area, looking for sites where they can graze.

Their search for food, such as grass, berries and seeds, will take place on dry land during the early morning, and around dusk.

May 13

The mute swan is the most common within Europe, and can be seen in an area covering the north west of the continent to the south east.
In some countries they are migratory, seeking unfrozen waters during the winter. However, the swans on Par Lake are mostly resident and in summer enjoy the warm, though frequently wet, Cornish weather.
The male grows to around 169 cm, with the female being around 14 cm shorter in length.

May 14

A pair of Canada geese preen themselves whilst in the background a heron hunts for tadpoles, frogs or small fish etc in the shallows near the reeds.
Usually, it is in April and May that a female heron lays four to five eggs. Then she, together with her mate, spend the following 25-28 days incubating them.
The birds rarely nest in the reeds, however, their choice site being high in trees.
On Par Lake the herons tend to build their nests in the trees on the island in the middle of the pool.
From there they have an excellent view of the lakeside and can probably spy the sea in the distance.

May 15

Four cygnets cluster together, feeling safe underneath their mother. Unfortunately, not all are to survive as the summer progresses. But by the end of the year many fully grown cygnets would have made the lake their home.
Swans do not fledge until they are about four and a half months old, while it takes four years for them to reach full maturity.

May 16

The wild roses blooming in the dunes are spreading, making the walk between the lake and the sea a growing riot of colour.

Over 100 species of wild rose grow in the British Isles, the most common of these being the dog rose which can grow to about 10' tall in some conditions.

Cultivated roses were bred from such plants as these, evolving over centuries from the wild to make gardens glorious.

May 17

There seems to be a Canada goose creche in operation here.

Families have probably joined together to help oversee the young as they gain in confidence and learn to graze the grass and search for food beneath the water—as, although they feed mostly on dry land, they do eat molluscs.

British birds are resident to the country, although in southern Sweden flocks will leave for Germany or Holland during the winter.

May 18

A female mallard swims happily around the lake on a May morning.

Female mallards, as elsewhere, are always in demand on the pool during the mating season, with some having around three male suitors following them around. In courtship the male lowers his bill, twitches his tail up and down, ruffles his feathers and then plunges his bill into the water.

May 19

A solitary cygnet takes a rest on the side of the lake, watched — just out of shot — by the pen.

In the background huddle a growing family of mallards who are catching up in size with their mother.

A cygnet can feed itself within 24 hours of hatching, its first swim taking place about the same time, as soon as it has dried out. Feeding usually takes place during the first swim, perhaps his, or her, parents pulling up algae, or maybe larvae, for this initial meal.

May 20

To some eyes Canadian goslings can look, initially, like ducklings as they are yellow and grey in colour with a dark bill. This changes after about seven days when their feathers gain more grey and the goslings themselves look a little more awkward.

Nine to ten weeks after hatching they are able to fly, having grown their flight feathers. They also bear much more than a passing resemblance to adult geese. This pair have one little gosling swimming behind them—one whose flight feathers have definitely yet to develop.

May 21

A jackdaw (*Corvus monedula*) sits cheekily on a post by the side of the lake, watching out for any scraps he, or she, can garner.

It is in April or May that individual pairs of jackdaws begin to build their nests, which can be found in crevices and hollows in a variety of places from old trees to edges of cliffs.

Straw, hairs and feathers are used to line the nest in which a clutch of five or six eggs will be laid.

Male and female jackdaws have a similar plumage and live off a diet of worms, molluscs, beetles and frogs etc.

May 22

A pied wagtail, a cheeky little character who prefers to live by a brook or pond, searches for insects by the side of the lake.
In summer pied wagtails (*Motacilla alba*) are very territorial, though not so in autumn and winter when they form large flocks.
In October and November such flocks choose to roost in the trees growing between the sand dunes and the lake.
The female has slightly more grey in her plumage than the male.

May 23

When they hatched these goslings, now 'old hands' among the lake's contingent, used an egg tooth, a projectile on their bill, to crack their shell.
As they hatched in down and were able to run, eat and swim within 24 hours, they are termed 'precocial'.
They learn, much the same as humans, by looking at the actions of their parents to amass knowledge about how to live and survive.
Feathers will start to replace their original down when they are about a month old.
.

May 24

Adding quiet tinges of blue to the surrounding countryside are the shy flowers of the speedwell.
The most common such flower is the Germander speedwell (*Veronica chamaedrys*) which flowers from March through until July.
The herb has flowers with four petals and opposite leaves.
The Germander speedwell grows in grassland and hedges, and has a white centre in its attractive flowers.

May 25

A clutch of caterpillars clings to one of the plants in the nearby sand dunes.

Those caterpillars, which will turn eventually into brown butterflies, are usually green and russet in colour, whilst those which are sited in obvious places, such as these, have spiny growths on them to deter predators from eating them. They have used glands in their bodies to secrete the raw materials for the silk that has bound them to the twig. This allows them to be secure while they grow and shed their skin as they do so.

May 26

A young wader sifts through the shallows after food, probably worms, crustaceans and small invertebrates.

The young of dunlin (*Calidris alpina*) and Common sandpiper have usually left their nest after about two days, but remain in the neighbourhood. Later, in the autumn, they will form flocks which roam the countryside seeking water. It is rare that such birds are actually seen swimming—they much prefer keeping their feet on solid ground.

May 27

Amidst lush green grass and a smattering of buttercups and daisies a Song thrush (*Turdus philomelos*) listens intently for the sound of activity below ground.

The young of this species leave the nest after about the fortnight, staying on the ground after that and continuing to be fed by both of their parents.

May 28

An expanse of yellow has broken out in the sand dunes, and the remainder of the land between the lake and sea. This has been a spell of welcoming, dry, warm weather—and the wild flowers have responded to it, covering the countryside in colour.

May 29

Against the backdrop of a brilliant blue sky a cluster of ox-eye daisies (*Chrysanthemum leucanthemum*) dances.
The leaves of this abundant wild flower are like those of a chrysanthemum, with the flowers having yellow centres to them.
They are also known as moon daisies and love to grow in old meadows and alongside railway embankments.
They can reach two foot in height in exposed places.

May 30

Mother may be close by, but these mallard ducklings are still keeping a close eye on her.
Ducklings are vulnerable to a range of predators, mainly because they are unable to fly away from an attack.
In the lake fish such as pike prove to be their prey, as well as birds such as herons.
Predators are also based on land, such as foxes, and in the air— hawks being one example.

May 31

The wild flowers continue to spread, studding the banks and the sand dunes, adding shades of colour, such as blue and lilac, to set off the fresh green of the summer grass.

June 1

The cygnets on the lake are growing up fast, as this youngster shows. The name 'cygnet' stems not only from the Middle English cignet, but also from the Anglo-Norman, diminutive cygne, and from the Latin cygnus.
When this cygnet's feathers have reached their full growth they will become dry, and not absorb water.

June 2

There are two species of iris which are native to Britain—the Yellow iris, as seen peeping through the reeds at Par—and the Stinking iris, or gladdon, which is found in southern England or on the Welsh coast, and which is purple in colour.
The Yellow iris will flower from May through to late July, and will grow up to two feet in height.
The Latin name of the Yellow iris is *Iris pseudacorus*.

June 3

The wild rhododendrons have started blooming, providing splashes of lilac around the beach.
The name rhododendron stems from the Greek 'rodon' which means rose, and 'dendro', meaning tree. There are more than 1000 species of this, Nepal's national flower.
Rhododendrons were initially introduced to Britain in 1656.

June 4

The flowers of the wild blackberries are out in the footpaths leading up to the beach.
Such plants as these can live for about 25 years. The flowers are mainly pollinated by bumblebees and honey bees.
Late spring and early summer are when the flowers are produced, each one having five white or pale pink petals.

June 5

Cygnets are sometimes seen riding on the backs of their parents, but this one is currently on land and just follows behind the parent bird instead.
Cygnets remain with the adult birds for about four or five months. Their colouring is usually a drab brown above and white below, but sometimes they are all-white.

June 6

A pair of mallards rest by the side of the lake, the distinction between the two still obvious, as the female remains much drabber.

However, when the male is in eclipse plumage later in the summer his general appearance will be similar to that of the female—as is the appearance of juvenile mallards.

June 7

Valerian is spreading alongside the verges leading up to the pool. Valerian, an ancient herb with a vanilla-like fragrance, was used by the Anglo-Saxons and Hippocrates. It is believed its name could stem from the Latin word 'valere' which means to be healthy, or from herbalist Valeris who believed in its medicinal properties.

It was introduced to Britain in the 16th century from southern Europe and loves to grow on old walls, in quarries and on cliffs.

June 8

A Lesser black-backed gull stands by the lakeside, on his own, distinctive against the other gulls by his size.

There are two types of black-backed gull—the Great (*Larus marinus*) and the Lesser (*Larus fuscus*).

Both types breed in colonies, often mingling alongside each other. They choose rocky coasts and islands (often in lakes) and marshy areas. Diets include fish, small birds and other birds' eggs.

June 9

It's been a warm day—so one of the visitors decides to take a plunge into the cool lake. Taking a dip is a labrador, not a resident of the pool! Those who are resident have made themselves very scarce.
Par beach is a favourite for dog lovers as there is no ban on four-legged friends—as long as everything they leave behind is bagged and binned.

June 10

As it moves along the dunlin feeds with a 'sewing machine' action, regularly and thoroughly sorting through food items, and choosing the best.
It prefers molluscs and worms and crustaceans in areas around the coast.
The commonest wader, the male has a distinctive black belly in the mating season, although in the winter the plumage is grey above and white below.

June 11

The buttercup, which carpets meadows throughout the UK, spreads through creeping runners. Its yellow flower, with its five petals, gleams like a jewel beside the bright green, hairy, leaves. A member of the *Ranunculaceae* family, it is a perennial flower which blooms from May through to August. The grass around the lake is bright with buttercups at the moment.

June 12

hese goslings seem happy
n the company of their
arents, but on occasion, if
'anada geese are seen, by
lder experienced adults, to
e lax parents their offspring
re often 'kidnapped'.
hese goslings are then
aised along with the more
xperienced pair's brood.
he original parents will be
llowed to stay with the
roup, but will be unable to
ke back their offspring.

June 13

A pair of rabbits are busy grazing
along one of the paths through
the sand dunes by the lake.
Although considered pests on
farmland they are regarded by
many as important in maintaining
the variety of habitats on dunes.
Their grazing helps prevent
brambles and other such scrubby
plants covering over habitats
which are rich with flowers.
Their burrows are often sited
under bramble bushes for
protection.

June 14

A splash of lilac catches the
eye—a Common
orchid (*Dactylorhiza fuchsii*),
which is one of the most
frequently spotted wild
orchids in the country.
Found in wooded and grassy
places it seems to enjoy both
sun or partial shade, although
acid soils are not to its liking.
It can be found both in
semi-natural and man-made
habitats, often gracing former
gravel pits, commons, heaths,
and railway embankments.

June 15

Flash floods hit the area, leading to quickly forming puddles by the lakeside.

Homes in Par, St Blazey and Carlyon Bay were affected by the flooding, which was up to 2' in some areas. Hailstones were described as falling 'like marbles'.

Traffic delays followed when the A3082 road at Par Docks became awash with rainwater.

June 16

The day after the thunderstorm the sun is out and the ducks are seeking shade rather than puddles. The wind has dropped, as shown by the calm surface of the lake and the clear reflection of the 'Deep Water' warning sign—which does not deter the ducks, of course.

June 17

The hen and cob are nearby, but this growing cygnet is quite comfortable in its own company.

Like the majority of the other lake dwellers the cygnet has little fear of visitors, rushing over to most of them in the hope that they bring food. Some of the swans, with cygnets in tow, will trail across to the car park, over the road, to 'mug' visitors as soon as they arrive in their vehicles.

June 18

The correct name of the small yellow slipper-like wild flower abundant at this time of year, in the hedges, is the bird's foot trefoil (*Lotus corniculatus*).
It is also known as bacon and eggs, fingers and thumbs and lady's slipper.
There are more than 70 names for the flower, which used to be woven into protective wreaths on Midsummer's Night, maybe because it is linked to the Holy Trinity.

June 19

There have probably been quite a few ducks released on the lake by pet owners or breeders, for a range of reasons.
This leads to interbreeding with the feral ducks who live there, especially the mallards.
The result is a number of hybrid ducks who produce fertile ducklings.
The genetic pool of a few wild mallards on the lake has probably been intermingled by both feral and domestic ducks. As a result, a few of their number have bright white fronts.

June 20

Wild magpies tend to be shy and wary, as opposed to tame birds which are likely to collect glittering items.
Magpies love hillsides covered by shrubs, woods and—as here—the edge of ponds.
Pairs build their nest in a tree or tall shrub in April, protecting this with a dome of thorny twigs.
Both parents feed the young for the first 24 days, continuing to do so for a while after they fledge.
Mice, insects, seeds, fruits and invertebrates make up their diet.

June 21

Midsummer's Day, and there is a green canopy in the lanes leading up to the lake.
Among this riot of green are abundant ferns, the fern being among the most primitive plants on the globe. Indeed, the fossils of ferns link back some 300 million years.
The perennial fern reproduces by means of spores, which appear between August and November and are spread through animals, and by the wind.
There are about 50 species of fern in Britain.

June 22

Small frogs are making their way along the paths towards water. They are tiny (like this little brown 'dot' at the bottom of the picture), about half an inch in length. They have changed from tadpoles, and so avoided being the prey of aquatic creatures such as newts and fish.
However, while growing they are likely to become the victim of herons, rats or hedgehogs etc.
Frogs are completely mature by the time they are three years of age.

June 23

A blackbird suns itself in the balmy air, stretching out its wings to feel the sun upon them.
Nearby, a rabbit stands and watches in the entrance to the brambles and undergrowth where no doubt it has its burrow.
Male blackbirds, during their first year, establish a territory which they will keep to for the rest of their lives.

June 24

Yellow wild flowers
bloom brightly against
the backdrop of an
azure sky.
Flowers are unfurling
along the sand dunes,
and in the hedges in the
warmth of the June sun.

June 25

One of the geese stands alone
for a moment, waiting for a
snack to be thrown.
At the moment the geese are
staying on or by the lake for
the majority of the day.
Later in the year they will
gather in groups to fly off for
hours during the day to graze
in surrounding fields.
Sometimes they will stay
away for the night, and fly
back to their main home the
next morning.

June 26

A young blackbird hides
in the undergrowth by
the pond, near one of its
parents.
Parents, in fact, feed
their offspring for up to
three weeks after they
leave the nest. They will
demonstrate their need
for food, by following
the adults, begging for a
snack.
Sometimes the female
will start another nest. If
this happens the male
will continue feeding the
youngsters on his own.

June 27

Making its way into the reeds is one of the lake's resident moorhens.
The birds breed in fresh water among thick cover, such as this reed bed, with the males fighting fiercely to defend their territory.
Such is the intensity in these fights that there have been reports of moorhens with dislocated thighs or even broken toes.

June 28

One of the female mallards is carrying out her maternal duties by the side of the lake.
Surrounded by her nine ducklings she demonstrates to them how to search for food—and all of them are doing as they are asked.
They are probably searching for minute piec-es from the stems of water plants.
The ducklings will fly at about six and a half weeks.

June 29

The thistles in the hedgerows are blooming. Altogether, there are 11 wild species of thistle which can commonly be found in Britain, ranging from the short carline thistle to the cotton thistle, which can grow to 6'.
The thistle's spikes protect it against grazing animals, while some insects lay their eggs in the axils of the leaves as the spikes protect them from predators.

June 30

Having fledged a young moorhen starts feeding for itself along the edges of the lake.

Moorhens start to lay their eggs between the middle of March and the middle of May.

The eggs are incubated for about 21 days, with both parents feeding the young which fledge after about 40-50 days, and become independent a little later.

July 1

The symmetry of nature is evident in the hedgerows.
Wild flowers pepper the grasses, bursting through to the sunlight to provide eye-catching natural patterns.

July 2

The flowers on many of the wild blackberries have been superseded by the fruits, which will gradually ripen over the coming weeks—changing from green, to red, to juicy black.

When ripe the fruit is picked for use in jams and seedless jellies etc.

There is a saying that the blackberry tends to be red when it is 'green' (relating to it still being unripe).

July 3

The flowers of the bindweed (*Convolvulus*) are gradually showing amongst the verdant vegetation near the pool.

There about 250 species of this plant, also known as Morning glory. Some are regarded as weeds, whilst others are specifically grown in gardens.

The trumpet-shaped flowers are usually white, or pink, but can also be blue, purple or yellow, depending on the specific species.

It is the main food plant for the caterpillars of the hawkmoth, a summer visitor to Britain.

July 4

Sunning itself in the foliage is a member of the *Satyrinae* family, Britain's small or medium brown butterflies which have eye-like spots on their wings.

This Speckled wood (*Pararge aegeria*), found in hedgerows and woods, has pale yellow markings on a brown background.

Some of the males can be very territorial, taking over areas and then defending them from intruders.

They love places where sunlight breaks through trees.

July 5

At home in the reeds is one of the lake's coots, carrying out its ablutions on its hidden nest.

A coot's nest is built from vegetation and sited in shallow water. It is usually hidden amongst vegetation, although sometimes is in the open.

The coot's large number of calls include a loud 'cut' sound which can be very distinctive.

July 6

The grasses and reeds along the riverbank are growing fast and high, curtaining the water with their richness.

Grasses are usually herbaceous plants while sedges are often associated with watercourses.

The family of sedges take in the papyrus sedge from which papyrus was formed in Ancient Egypt, as well as cotton-grass.

This part of the watercourse in Par is where a kingfisher is often spotted, a blue iridescent flash which skims down the river towards the wild area below the cliffs.

July 7

The flower of the honeysuckle is forming part of the floral backdrop around the pool.

The honeysuckle is renowned for its beauty, fragrance and medicinal qualities.

It also provides somewhere to hide and feed for bees and insects etc. Moths are especially attracted to its nectar.

In the time of Shakespeare it was known by another name—that of woodbine.

There are garden varieties which are held in high esteem.

July 8

An egret stands in the small reed island, listening for sounds beneath the water.

Its name stems from French, from the word 'aigrette' which highlights the long plume the bird develops in the breeding season.

This led to them being hunted to the brink of extinction in past years, as the long feathers were sought by hat makers in Europe and the United States.

This demand meant that the birds were sought out and killed in the breeding season.

July 9

Two hybrid mallards swim lazily in the middle of the lake.

Mallards are one species which seem to mate with ease with differing species of duck.

At Par the white-fronted ducks, with typical iridescent mallard feathers in their plumage, mix quite happily with each other.

July 10

A juvenile black-headed gull stands by the side of the pool, slightly away from the large number of adults.

The black-headed gull breeds early in the year, with many of the young birds already flying by the middle of June.

In their juvenile plumage the birds have a crown, neck and mantle with brownish feathers. By early winter these will have disappeared.

They are very sociable birds and can often be seen feeding with other types of gulls or lapwings.

July 11

A male stonechat, with his distinctive black head, orange-red breast and the white around his neck, perches on his own on the low bushes leading up to the lake.

The females are less striking, as they do not have the black heads, and their chests only have an orange tinge.

Its name is derived from the sound it makes—like two stones being tapped together.

July 12

A member of the *Nymphalidae* family, which takes in about 5000 species of butterflies, has alighted on the flowering hedgerow.

Mostly medium to large in size these butterflies have colourful wings, although some of their under wings are much duller. This can provide a form of camouflage, helping them merge into their surroundings.

July 13

Some scientists believe there is evidence that Canada geese communicate with differing sounds—perhaps up to 13 of them.

These will, of course, include greetings and warnings, as well as sounds of happiness. It is thought that goslings are still in the egg when they begin communicating with their parents.

On the lake a number of calls are being made between this flotilla of geese.

July 14

Ragwort, a plant which is poisonous to animals, is starting to flower in the hedgerows and sand dunes.

This plant, which horse lovers hate due to its poisonous 'qualities', is also known as Stinking Nanny, Cankerwort and Stammerwort etc.

Bees, moths, insects and butterflies pollinate ragwort, which is biennial or perennial.

July 15

Gulls go through a number of plumages as they turn from juvenile into adult birds.
The smaller gulls take two years to go through the transition, but larger, medium sized birds take three years and those who are larger still a whole four years.
This Par pool youngster seems exceptionally proud of his current plumage.

July 16

The leaves of the sycamore trees, growing along the bank of the stream which leads to the sea, are a rich green.
Recent rain has left the stream a brown colour, due to the amount of mud which has been washed into it.
The name of the tree is linked to the fig species, referred to in the Bible, because of their supposedly similarly shaped leaves.
The tree can easily stand both wind and salt spray.

July 17

Butterflies and moths are making the most of the warmer weather, and alighting on the wild flowers growing all around the lake.
Many of them spread their wings to bathe in the sun's rays.
A walk around the pool, and then on to the cliff path as it winds around the coast to the beach at nearby Polkerris, will allow the rambler to note a rich wealth of nature, including the range of butterflies and moths.

July 18

A moth, probably a Wood Tiger moth, hides away in the grass, almost disguising itself from residents, or holidaymakers, as they wander around the pond, through the dunes and onto the long, sandy beach which attracts so many to Par.

The wildlife also proves to be a draw. The male Wood Tiger moth is frequently found by day on ground vegetation.

July 19

A line of mute swans march across the grass, probably heading towards food.

At the end of this month swans usually become flightless because of the moulting of their feathers.

This state will last for around six weeks. At Abbotsbury Swannery advantage is taken of their lack of flight to round them up and weigh and examine them, as well as ring newcomers.

The swans may have increased at Par but not to the 600 or so that can be found at Abbotsbury.

July 20

Around this time of year, in July and August, robins are seldom seen or heard because they are moulting and tend to hide away. However, at other times they sing throughout the night.

On occasions, due to their determined and melodious song in the hours of darkness, they have been mistakenly identified as a nightingale.

July 21

Two young mallards stay close to their mother as they start exploring their surroundings.
While some of this year's ducklings have begun to assert themselves amongst the inhabitants these are quite newly hatched and remain hesitant regarding venturing far on their own.
The male has played his part now, and is not to be seen!

July 22

Wild apples grow from a tree shading one of the footpaths that will eventually take the walker up to the pool.
The tree could have been cultivated, or grown as the result of a thrown away apple core.
There are a few such trees to be found in the outskirts of the beach and lake, their fruits probably very edible.
Insects or bees are needed to cross-pollinate apple trees, honey bees being among the most successful such pollinators.
When mature, apple trees can reach up to 12 metres in height. although usually they are smaller.

July 23

A moorhen makes its way across the water.
Moorhens can often have up to three broods a year, but are quite well known for 'losing' their clutches of eggs.
The birds from the first brood sometimes feed and protect younger members of the family from later broods. This is because they tend to stay close to the nesting site.
However, when they are more than old enough to look after themselves the father tries to chase the male adolescents away from the area.

July 24

Cygnets grow slower than the young of other swimming birds, and stay close to their parents for much longer.

At night they sleep in the nest with their mother, and stay with their parents for around two years.

In this time they absorb knowledge about migration routes.

Some stay as long as it takes for them to find a mate.

July 25

Hidden amongst the ivy and grasses is a bee, industriously seeking nectar.

This was a summer when concern was shown about dwindling numbers of bees, whether it be due to spreading disease, use of chemicals or destruction of habitat.

The majority of bees across the world are solitary, with about 270 such species.

As solitary bees prefer a specific flower, their life ends when the flower's season finishes—as their food supply has ended.

July 26

Along the paths and around the pool the odd wildflower is beginning to develop a seed head.

This prompts thoughts that, although it is the height of the summer, autumn is just around the corner.

The leaves remain fresh green, with the trees in full leaf.

However, signs of the next season are now in creeping evidence.

July 27

The trees throw shadows on the grass as the sun beams down on Par beach and its surrounding areas, including the lake.
The leaves are now showing summer green and are just starting to display their fruits which will gradually ripen as the season eases its way towards autumn.

July 28

The blackberries, especially those in sunny positions, are gradually ripening.
They are ideal for jams and jellies, as well as blackberry and apple crumble. However, country lore explains that they should be picked before Michaelmas, which occurs on September 29.
They should not be foraged after this date as, it is said, the devil would have claimed them as his after then.
Overall, they are renowned for their nutritional benefits, as they include vitamins and antioxidants.

July 29

The rain has continued to fall, leaving the pool brown with mud and forming puddles on the verges which then flood into the nearby road.
The mallards have abandoned the pool and decided instead to cluster around the flooded grass.
Surface-feeding mallards love to dabble in shallow water or filter through soft mud, such as this, for their food.
They love the seeds of aquatic plants, and grains although aquatic invertebrates are also enjoyed, especially during the breeding season.

July 30

Flowers and shrubs have sprung up between the dunes and the pool, providing another habitat for birds, insects and animals.
Again, fruits and flowers are evident, as is cover for those who want to establish nests or burrows hidden away from the prying eyes of those humans who wander through the dunes on their way to the beach, and the sea.

July 31

A drowsy day. The geese are gathering together in the pool, readying themselves for their flight to nearby fields, where they will feed on grass overnight.
Then they will return in squadron formation the following day.
Ahead of their departure the geese make a combined noise that resonates across to the beach.

August 1

A young moorhen saunters along by the side of the pool, quite happy in its own company now that it has forged its independence from the nest.
On the whole moorhens enjoy feeding by the edge of the water, and are more solitary birds than coots, with whom they are often confused.
The chicks have black, downy feathers although not around the eye and bill. Juveniles, such as this one, have browner under parts.

August 2

The sycamore, known as the plane tree in Scotland, grows throughout the British Isles. It was introduced to the country in the 17th century.

In Scotland there are links with Mary Queen of Scots as she was meant to have helped her husband, Lord Darnley, recover from illness while they were resting under a plane tree.

Its Latin name is *Acer pseudoplatanus.*

August 3

Swans are such excellent parents that a cygnet on its own can mean that trouble is afoot.

Young cygnets are vulnerable, although this one is now growing in size and awareness. Parental control remains strong, however, and a watchful eye is kept on the youngster as further exploration of the pool is made.

August 4

Despite it being the height of the summer season the rain has continued falling, leading to high water levels remaining around the pool.

A watery sun glistens on the water between a break in the clouds. Oblivious to the despair of sun-seekers, the swans and ducks paddle around peacefully.

August 5

Hidden amongst the drying grasses on the coast path leading from the pool is a burnet moth, resplendent in its colours of black and red. Although most moths prefer the darkness, burnets choose to come out during the daytime.

There is a reason for this because they are unlikely to be eaten by birds because they taste terrible and are also slightly poisonous.

August 6

The bright berries of the wild arum or cuckoo pint (*Arum maculatum*) are evident in the hedgerows, signalling that autumn is on its way.

These berries are formed from the plant's lower ring of female flowers. Much of the rest of the plant has by now withered away.

The berries are poisonous and can cause a burning sensation in the mouth if eaten.

August 7

Two Painted lady butterflies (*Vanessa cardui*) have alighted on grass and thistle.

The Painted lady butterfly is most often seen around late summer. Its upper wings are a buff-orange colour near its body, with different markings—dark brown and black with white patches—nearer the edges of its wings.

It is one of the largest to be seen in the UK and, although most common in August, can be spotted throughout other months in the year.

August 8

A Meadow brown butterfly suns itself near the lake. Meadow browns can be found in a large range of habitats, but do enjoy residing in coastal dunes and where the grasses shoot up high.

They much prefer areas where the grass will not be cut and the nectar continues to abound.

They will fly when the weather is dull, unlike many of their contemporaries.

August 9

A mallard shelters amongst the wild flowers by the side of the lake, hiding her new brood of ducklings.

The initial brood of mallards usually appear in the latter half of April, the majority hatching between then and July. However, if a nest is destroyed and re-nesting takes place further broods can be raised, sometimes as late as August.

August 10

While some flowers are still blooming, others are now dying back, depending on the temperature.

Flowering for some wild flowers continues through August, until the initial frosts of the season, but not for these. Their seeds are forming while many are still on their summer holidays.

An example is this dying plant which stands out amongst a background which remains an overall green.

August 11

If in its normal habitat
this Bar-headed goose
may have been starting
to consider a migration
route over the Himalayas
to India, Assam,
Northern Burma or
Pakistan. There it would
feast on barley, wheat or
rice.

However, a different
migration route may be
considered by this Par
goose.

August 12

Summer days, a sunny
morning, and the
mallards and mallard
crosses, are finding
that life is one lazy,
hazy doze.

The mating season is
past, the ducklings on
the lake are establishing
their presence, there are
enough holidaymakers
providing seed, and the
world is to be enjoyed.
Relaxation is king.

August 13

The thistles in the hedgerows are
showing signs of impending autumn as
their purple flowers give way to seeds.
The thistle, the national emblem of
Scotland, stands for the era when the
Scots were fighting the Norsemen, who
landed on the coast of their
enemies.

They tried to creep inland silently,
removing their boots to do so.
However, one of them stepped on a
sharp thistle and the resulting scream
alerted the Scots soldiers who, up until
then, had been sleeping.

The invaders were hunted down, and
beaten.

August 14

A snail snuggles down on the leaf of a wild honeysuckle plant, growing within feet of the lake.
If lucky, snails can live from between five and ten years. The oldest one ever found was aged 15 and the largest measured 15 inches and weighed two pounds.
However, this example, trying to find the coolest spot in the hedgerow, is much smaller.

August 15

The sky is full of black-headed gulls, all after one kind of prey—the flying ant.
As the ants take to the big wide world the gulls are up above, just waiting for them.
High above them are swifts, waiting for those insects which safely fly through the barrage of gulls.
It is believed that at this time of year certain weather conditions trigger the ants' mating behaviour which leads them to head for the skies—and the beaks of waiting birds.

August 16

The bright green leaves of those trees leading up to the lake are turning darker as the days edge towards autumn.
Berries are gradually forming, and turning from green to a red which heralds the change of seasons. The saying goes that the more berries around the colder the winter ahead will be.
There is the hint, from the berries forming, that cold days are ahead.

August 17

The flowering period of the bulrush, or greater reed-mace is August to December. Those growing along the edges of the lake at Par are already peeking through the reeds.

The male flower is straw coloured whilst the female flower is darker and more cylindrical.

The seed heads remain intact during the winter, but explode to let the seeds free in spring.

August 18

A female mallard swims alongside her newly hatched duckling—a bundle of fluff much smaller than the ducklings hatched so much earlier in the year. Only female mallards quack, as the males whistle and grunt instead.

It is thought that the mallard was the first domesticated bird, domesticated even before the chicken.

August 19

Summer is nearing its end, autumn is in the wings and the trees are starting to rest, deciding to survive on food stored during the long, hot, sunny days. Green chlorophyll in the leaves starts to disappear and the yellow and red colours, which have been within the leaves all the time, begin to become distinctive.

.

August 20

The adult Canada geese on the lake start to moult. This is an annual occurrence when their goslings have reached about a month or more of age.

During this time of their life they cannot fly for around four or five weeks. Their feathers begin to return about the same time as the goslings learn to fly.

Flight feathers, from those who moult, start to return around September, now not many weeks away at all.

.

August 21

Wild flowers continue to abound around the lake. Among them is a member of the mallow family (*Malvaceae)* of which there are around 2,800 species around the globe.

The species takes in cotton plants producing fibres for textiles and oil which is extracted from their seeds, as well as ornamental species such as rose-of-sharon.

Okra and hibiscus are also members of this extensive family.

August 22

A fungus peeps through the grass by the side of the lake, this a harbinger of autumn.

Fungus stems from the Latin word meaning mushroom.

It occurs in the writings of Horace and Pliny.

It is thought that the study of fungi in England began in the 19th century.

August 23

Loud discussions take place amongst the goose population.

For those living near the pool the sound of geese has become a common background noise.

The geese are at their loudest when taking off from the water to fly to surrounding fields to graze. Debates on when to take off as a unit can develop into quite a screeching discussion.

August 24

The blackberries are starting to ripen, especially those near the lake in sites which receive the greatest amount of sunshine. Now is the time when they will start to be gleaned from the hedgerows, to be eaten fresh or maybe frozen for use later in the year.

August 25

Resting by the lake in the sunshine are two of the resident ducks.

There is a drowsy, late summer feel to the day, reflected by these two who are obviously well fed and happy to just watch the world go by.

Autumn is waiting in the wings, but today is being kept very much at bay still.

August 26

Leaves are strewn on the grass by the pool after the tail end of Hurricane Bill swept into the South West.

The deep frontal depression brought with it, following its journey across the Atlantic, gale force winds and rain.

Cruise liner visits were cancelled further west, and visitors and residents had to batten down the hatches.

Residents of the lake also made themselves scarce.

August 27

The robin feeds mostly on worms and insects, which it snatches from the ground after watching out for movement from a perch of their choice.

They also, craftily, keep their eye on gardeners who are tilling the ground, following behind for anything they can easily eat.

Robins also enjoy any food which is left out by bird lovers, such as the seed left on this rock on the entrance to Par Beach.

Fruit cake, uncooked pastry and mealworms are also favourite dishes.

August 28

A solitary crow wades in the gently lapping water on the edge of the lake.

The crow is a member of the *Corvidae* family which also includes colourful jays, and rooks.

Some believe crows initially evolved in Asia, from birds who had originated in Australia.

Crows frequently seem to enjoy their own company, although a group of them are called a 'murder' of crows.

A wader searches for food by the water's edge.
The bird, who looks like a juvenile, is surrounded by debris blown from the surrounding land, and the lake, following the recent high winds.
The weather is still today and the residents of the pool are more in evidence.

August 30

Mist and rain shroud the lake in the middle of which a heron stands patiently, waiting for its next meal.
Herons mainly feed on fish but they also eat amphibians, small mammals and, occasionally, birds.
They will wait happily for their prey to make itself readily available.
After the young are hatched both the adult parents will feed them.

August 31

A cygnet stays close to its parents, despite its rapidly increasing size.
Breeding will not start for this bird until it is around three years old.
When it does eventually nest a clutch of around three and seven eggs will be laid, although up to 13 have been recorded.
The eggs are usually laid over a two day period.

September 1

A rainbow is clearly visible above the lake, spearing out from behind the fields on the horizon. Rainbows were seen as a promise made between Earth and Heaven, whilst myths have claimed they represented the bow of the God of Love, a bow of war, or a link between the lives of the gods and humankind.

September 2

The swans, and one of the cygnets, seek out the puddles left by continuous driving rain.

A severe rain warning was issued by the Met Office for Cornwall as heavy grey clouds swept across the county, swamping the countryside with 15-20mm of water.

Drivers were warned to take extra care, especially on flooded main roads.

None of this bothered the swans, sifting through the standing water for food.

September 3

Gulls are voracious creatures, able to feast on a variety of food and smart enough to know instantly when the farmer is ploughing or the fisherman has located a shoal. Apart from feeding on aquatic life they also enjoy worms, insects, eggs and berries, as well as small animals.

Landfill sites attract them as they will try to eat a variety of human garbage. However, this juvenile's attempt to eat the discarded sole of a shoe is bound to fail!

September 4

A dragonfly alights on one of the dry reeds by the side of the Par Beach lake. Dragonflies can be found from sea level, right up to mountains, although their numbers fall as the altitude increases. They are related to mayflies and damselflies.
A large number of the adult dragonflies have metallic colours, or very bright iridescent ones, although those who have freshly emerged as adults usually have paler colours that then become brighter.
They often defend their territory and choose perches which have an excellent view over their favoured feeding areas.
It is said that the female dragonflies can pretend to be dead in order to avoid unwanted interest from males.

September 5

Many leaves, especially those in the dampest areas, still harbour a bright summer green. Today the sun is out and the bugs and insects are making the most of the temperatures, either gathering late summer nectar, or bathing in the sun's rays.

There is a hope that this year may have an Indian summer, but whether that happens or not depends on the coming days.

September 6

One of the lake's juvenile gulls is gradually growing its adults feathers.

A gull will, throughout its life, go through moults in both autumn and spring. In summer it will have its alternate plumage and in winter its basic plumage. The autumn moult, apart from the initial one, will see a moult of all feathers while the spring moult sees feathers lost from the body but not the wings and tail.

September 7

There remain a number of mallard hybrids on the lake—which is not at all unusual.

Among other breeds the mallards frequently mate with are species such as the pintail.

One of the many ducks with mallard features, but with bright white fronts, settles by the lakeside for a September siesta.

September 8

Purple flowers peep out from the green to bring continuing colour to sides of the footpaths leading to the lake.

Late summer sunshine is reflected on the leaves, and brings warmth to an area which has seen enough of the rain over the very damp previous weeks.

September 9

A sparrow makes the most of seed left out for the wild birds on one of the granite rocks.

Shyer than the cheeky House sparrow, the bird blends into the surroundings.

Sparrows are thought to have originated in Africa. Although they like wooded environments they have adapted well to domesticated areas.

September 10

A line of Canada geese are busy preening in the sun, helping to keep their feathers clean and dry.

They pull each feather individually, taking off the dirt. Shaking and ruffling the feathers gets rid of excess water and lets air flow into them. The birds' bills are then used to get oil from the oil gland at the base of the tail, and rub it all over the feathers.

September 11

Canada geese line the lake, gathering in families, preening, sunbathing or eating.
Their main diet is of green vegetation and grains. They eat a variety of grasses, grasping a blade with their bill and then tearing it out of the ground with a skilled jerk of their head.
Grains such as wheat, rice and corn are enjoyed, as well as aquatic plants such as seaweed.

September 12

Only a few British coots will leave the country in the coming months for warmer climes.
On the whole most of them will remain, probably including this one, forming flocks on reservoirs or at gravel pits.
Other birds will then join them, flying in from Scandinavia to add to the numbers. With winter still in the wings, however, this coot is just busy snoozing.

September 13

This Bar-headed goose is a long way from Mount Everest, but every spring flocks of these birds, the highest altitude migrants in the world, fly from their winter feeding grounds through the Himalayan mountains to Tibet, where they nest. Their route can take them directly over Everest.
In fact it is thought they can fly the 1000 miles between India and Tibet in 24 hours.

September 14

The elderberries are now ripe and obvious in the hedgerows.
They are a great favourite of wild birds, and are said to have health benefits for humans as well—although it's probably not advisable to eat the berries when they are red, or uncooked. When cleaned and cooked, however the berries can form syrup and be put in pies or perhaps used to make elderberry wine!

.

September 15

The reeds whisper along the riverbank in the September breeze.
Reeds usually grow in less than l metre of water, most species having aerial shoots which emerge in spring green earlier in the year. They can grow to up to three metres, and then die back in the autumn.
Silt is trapped around the shoots in shallow water, altering river flow and allowing the plant to spread further.

September 16

A cormorant, which has made the island in the middle of the lake his home, stands on a rock, perhaps waiting to dive into the water for a fish. Cormorants tend to nest in colonies, using trees, rocky islets or cliffs to gather together.
There seems to be ancient ties to the cormorant, with similar ancestors tied to the era of the dinosaurs.

September 17

Berries are starting to be in greater evidence in the hedgerows, paving the way for autumn. Their colours vary from yellow through to black.
The berries will provide a staple food for birds in the coming months, although some gardeners believe they prefer red and orange berries to those which are black or blue.

September 18

Feathers are strewn alongside the edge of the lake, blown by an increasing autumn wind.
The weather has turned colder and the ducks are sheltering under nearby bushes, out of the weather, rather than gathering around the lake's edge.

September 19

A heron once again stands patiently by the edge of the pool, persevering in its quest for food.
Herons feature widely in sayings and mythology.
It was said that, when predicting weather, rain is due when a heron is seen flying low, while fine weather is approaching if the flight line is high.

September 20

Hay is being gathered in the fields above the lake, while the swallows seem to have disappeared.
Swallows seen in Britain in summer spend their winter in South Africa, flying across the Pyrenees, through Spain, Morocco and then across the Sahara into West Africa, although some divert around the Sahara.

September 21

Lilac daisies peep out from the grasses and weeds continuing to flourish by the side of the water.
Although the sides and tips of the leaves are starting to turn brown, in acknowledgement of oncoming autumn, there is a warm, summery feel to the weather that was absent on some days in August.

September 22

Berries continue to ripen in the hedges.
The saying goes that the more berries the greater the likelihood of a harsh winter ahead.
It is nature's way of supplying enough food for wildlife— helping the birds to survive cold weather which leads to frozen soil.
For now, though, winter seems to be more than a while hence.

September 23

The fruit of the sycamore tree is ball-shaped and fully ripens in October. The fruit is woody and keeps its shape throughout the winter before breaking up into dozens of tiny seeds that feature tiny brown hairs. They are then scattered by the wind.

September 24

There is a peaceful gathering of gulls and terns by the side of the lake.
Today there is no squabbling over food, just a feeling of camaraderie on the shoreline.
The 'beach' which has formed shows that water levels are certainly below those evident in wetter periods.

September 25

A spell of Indian summer has arrived with blue skies, warm winds and a last hurrah for those who enjoy sunny weather - whether they be human or feathered.
There is a lot of activity on the lake, a swirling of wings and dipping of beaks and bills in the water.

September 26

Leaves are falling from the trees rapidly, stripping the branches of cover as they do so. The result is almost bare branches which weave a lacy patchwork against a bright blue sky. The trees form a line between the lake and the nearby car park from which visitors watch the pool's inhabitants.

September 27

Beautiful weather bathes the lake. In the distance a flotilla of geese lazily swim near the far reeds, while on land a quartet of coots search for food. The sun casts their silhouettes against the grass while they forage. Behind them the white breasts of two gulls shine in the warm rays.

September 28

Seeds are forming as the flowers gradually die away. The weather is still today, which means winds will not start to distribute the seeds around the dunes— but over the coming weeks that will change. The flowers may be dying but the process is all part of the continuing life of the lake and its surroundings.

September 29

There has been a long, dry spell but the absence of long, light days has meant that the leaves have lost their green and turned a variety of autumnal colours.
They have also fallen from the trees and now carpet the green grass, blowing across towards the lake.

September 30

Amongst the seeding thistle heads and the dying flowers, petals are still poking through the hedgerows, brightening up the clumps of briars and drying bracken.
The recent dry weather has meant that there have been sunny corners where summer seems to be trying to hang on as long as possible.

October 1

The absence of rain for the past weeks has meant that the level of the water has dropped dramatically.
Not long ago the 'Beware Deep Water' sign was standing in water—not so now. The gulls and geese have been scavenging in the exposed mud.

October 2

A pair of jackdaws search for insects near the lake side. The jackdaw is the smallest of the crows. These intelligent, inquisitive birds are all black as adults apart from grey on their shoulders and round their ears. Their eyes are almost white, although they are brown until the bird's first autumn.

October 3

By now the young Canada geese have gone through their moult and so are able to take to the air.
As a result, the family as a whole can fly, joining with other geese to form large flocks which can move from the lake to nearby fields to graze.

October 4

Dew has formed in sparkling droplets on one of the now leafless trees near the lake. It is early morning and the dew has formed from water which condensed on the cool surface of the tree overnight, from water vapour in the air.

October 5

The cygnets are growing, this one almost the same size as its parents now.
Male mute swans are larger than females, and the knob at the base of their upper bill is larger as well.
The neck of a male is also thicker than that of a female.

October 6

The Bar-headed goose seems to be a resident at the moment, happily flying with a flock of the others when they visit nearby fields to graze. Having returned from one of their sojourns the geese have settled once more on the lake, with their Himalyan friend among them.

October 7

The daisies are still in flower, adding a patch of cheery white and yellow around one of the local granite stones. The daisy does not, in fact, flower all year round as there is usually a period in deepest winter when this most common of Britain's wildflowers is absent from fields and lawns.

October 8

Evening sun lights up the bushes and reeds around the edge of the lake.

The day has been warm for the time of year, and still. The Canada geese are grazing on the grass leading down to the water's edge. There is no breeze to ruffle the surface of the pond, which is reflecting the colours of the season.

October 9

A new cygnet has arrived to add to the lake's inhabitants. It has slightly darker feathers than the resident cygnets but is about the same size.

The newcomer could be a cygnet which has previously been living in Par River which flows into the sea at the far end of the beach.

October 10

The bracken in the hedgerows is now brown and decaying, in contrast to nearby leaves which remain a fresh green,

If collected in autumn dead bracken can be rotted down to make mulch in a similar way to leaves being used to make leaf mould for the garden.

October 11

A pair of mallards paddle happily near the edge of the lake, forming ripples which spread out around them.
The ducklings of the spring and summer have been hatched and raised and parental duties have now eased away.

October 12

Ivy, still a bright green, twists its way around the vegetation, bushes and trees around the pond.
Its umbrella-like clusters of flowers, which are yellowish green in colour, open in September, while the fruits harden through the winter, being blue initially, before turning black.

October 13

Both wasps and bees can be found making the area around the pond their home.
There are, of course, differences between the species. Bees collect pollen but wasps do not.
Bees store food, while wasps do not and bees make honey which wasps fail to do.
The nests of wasps are made of paper, and those of bees of wax.

October 14

Lichens dot the trunk and branches of the now leafless trees.
Often lichens are so small, and blend so well into their host plant, it is difficult to notice them. Trees are one of the best places for lichens to flourish, as well as on the fringe of rocky beaches and in old graveyards.

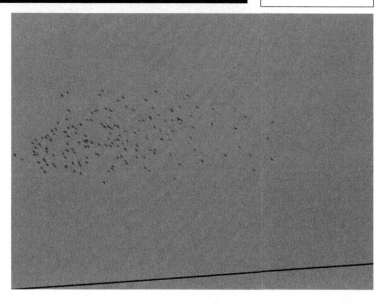

October 15

Geese fly back to the lake after grazing in the farmers' fields nearby. During autumn the geese enjoy eating acorns, a good source of protein for their diet. At this time of year they also devour leaves which have fallen onto the ground. Another factor they need in their diet is gravel.

October 16

As soon as dusk starts to gather the starlings appear in the darkening skies over the lake. One by one small groups of the passerines meet until they have formed a spectacular feathered cloud—a murmuration of starlings.
Migrant and resident birds are meeting to forage before they roost together in the reeds.

October 17

The swans, and a cygnet, gather together to tuck into some food which has been left on the grass by the side of the lake.

This is a very crafty method of eating, as it prevents any other resident of the pond getting a snack too!

The geese and the ducks can only look on as they have no chance of gate-crashing the party.

October 18

Seagulls fly seawards as dusk starts to fall.

They gather in the skies above Par, making their way over the sand-dunes and out towards the ocean.

Their cries echo in the air, filling all around with their sounds.

October 19

A dry spell has meant that very little rain has fallen over the last few days and, as a result, the pond levels are not that high at the moment.

Canada geese have taken off from the water and are flying off to find grass to graze.

They fly in squadrons, this quite large one heading over to the fields on the surrounding cliffs to discover lush pickings.

October 20

One of the terns stands on the grass which surrounds the pond, surveying all around him. The common 'family' name, *Sterna*, may be from the Old English, and a poem written around 1000 AD.

October 21

Autumn is usually regarded as the season for fungi—and it is true that they are at their most evident at this time of year. Nevertheless, individual species have their own season, but they tend to overlap more during autumn.

Indeed, some only appear in the spring or prefer the summer. The oyster mushroom appears in the winter.

October 22

A rainbow arc shoots across the sky from the hills behind the pond. The sky is a darkening grey and the clouds far from light and fluffy, but the colours of the rainbow brighten the scene.

The inhabitants of the pond seem mainly to have hidden themselves away in the reeds.

October 23

It is high tide, as evident by the water seeping from the lake into the verdant edges surrounding it.
The grass remains green and fresh, as do the leaves from surrounding plants, which appear to be keeping the depths of autumn at bay— for a while at least.

October 24

The first winter plumage of gulls starts showing in September, when they undergo their initial moult and start growing new feathers. This first moult in the autumn is only a partial one as they retain their wing and tail feathers. There is a real group of younger gulls gathering together today.

October 25

A crow stands on one of large rocks which were put in place to form a channel into the harbour at Par.
Crows are omnivorous and will eat anything, from earthworms to frogs and young birds to molluscs.
Some crows can live to the age of 20—one wild crow in America known to have lived to almost 30.

October 26

There has been misty weather throughout the day, but this heron can be easily seen as it stands patiently on the edge of the lake, waiting for that one movement that will highlight the presence of a fish, fit for plunder. Ducks swim around the heron, one of a family which live happily on the island in the middle of the water.

October 27

Two cygnets wander around on the grass between the lake and the caravans and chalets in the local holiday park. They seem to have formed a bond as two young swans on the lake and appear quite happy in the surroundings which have been theirs since emerging from their separate eggs.

October 28

The amount of starlings making up the local murmuration is gradually growing, which means that their appearance over the lake and surrounding cliffs and fields becomes more impressive each evening. The starlings gradually gather over a period of about 45 minutes, with small groups joining at regular intervals, until they all suddenly swoop into the reeds, where they then roost.

October 29

Autumnal colours are very evident now as the leaves slowly die away, their fresh and strident greens changing through yellow and red hues to brown.
As the wind strengthens they whisper in the growing breeze and then flutter to the ground forming ever-growing natural carpets.

October 30

Pampas grass (*Cortaderia selloana*) is growing in the nearby sand-dunes, standing tall above surrounding vegetation. Native to South America its name stems from the pampas on which it naturally grows. It can reach to a height of three metres and its leaves can be silvery grey but are also a bluish-green colour.

October 31

Halloween—but there are no witches flying across the lake this evening. Instead, a squadron of geese have taken off from the lake and are flying off to find grass to graze on in nearby fields.
They usually announce that they are about to take off by honking loudly, as if giving each other flight instructions.

November 1

Par and the surrounding area were hit by gales overnight, but the winds eventually abated and the swans ventured out onto the lake again.
The village sited high above Par is that of Tywardreath which appeared in the Domesday Book, but as spelt Tiwardrai.
A Benedictine priory was once sited here, but it was dismantled in 1540.
The sea water once reached up to Tywardreath through what is now a green valley.

November 2

Grey clouds continue to sweep over the Cornish countryside, coastline and Par harbour. On the lake swans gather together for company.
A couple of hundred years before the harbour was built Roundhead soldiers, who had just been defeated in a battle at Castle Dore, an Iron Age hill fort outside Fowey, fled to nearby coves and beaches to escape by sea.
The Royalists had been victorious, but this was one of the last battles they won in the conflict.

November 3

Pine cones can be gathered during the autumn in the UK, these being the woody fruiting body and reproductive organ of pine trees, such as those around the Par Beach lake.
There are three native conifers in the UK, these being the Scots pine which has the traditional pine cones, the juniper which produces cones with tiny scales and the yew whose cones resemble red, fleshy, berries.

November 4

Light shines through the evergreen trees that dominate the edge of the lake, and onto the swathe of ivy below. The evergreens provide cover for the smaller birds who nest there in spring, and, when it's raining, for the water birds who want to 'escape' the lake now and then.

November 5

The loud murmuration of starlings, that gathers every evening over the reed beds is growing larger day by day.
Such sights can turn the sky darker as the birds swoop and glide in unison.

November 6

Silhouetted against a grey sky are wild plants that have flowered in previous months and are now past their glory.
Gradually, the vegetation is dying away, and the flowers are fading.

Evidence that the weather has been damp is there for all to see in the depth of the puddles and the water seeping into the grass on the edges of the pond. Reflections of foliage shimmer on the rising water levels, adding to the lake's attraction.

November 8

Wind whipping across the pond ensures that waves are as evident there, as they are out to sea.
Swans swim against the 'tide', as do a number of the resident ducks, bobbing up and down as they do so. The sun is shining, however, as shown by the gull's shadow.

November 9

The weather today has been excellent for this time of year, leaving an ideal late autumn evening.
Lights from the homes lining the road between Par and Fowey are reflected on the water.
A family of swans throw up elegant, almost ghostly appearances.

November 10

Silver birch trees, growing near the lake, can be seen in silhouette as dusk falls. These are deciduous trees, and before their new leaves appear in the spring the twigs will turn a reddish-purple colour. The new leaves will be evident around April and will initially be a bright green, which will gradually darken before becoming yellow, or brown, in autumn months.

On a Silver birch these leaves turn a brighter yellow than on a Downy birch. It is late October, early November when the leaves begin to tumble.

November 11

One of the resident lighter coloured ducks mingles with those mallards of more standard plumage.

In the face of a strong wind, and gloomy rain, they are choosing to keep together by the side of the water, rather than take to the lake.

November 12

The wet spell continues, ensuring that the water levels keep rising.

The grassy edges by the reeds, usually home to families of rabbits as evening encroaches, are now so sodden that any further rain just serves to extend the size of the lake itself.

November 13

Leaves carpet the ground lying between the lake and the sea – leaves of all colours, from russets to browns, and fading yellows. However, some leaves still bravely cling to trees, sparkling silver as the wind blows through them.

November 14

A blackbird sings in the bare branches of a tree whose roots, usually on dry land, are now enclosed by water. Male blackbirds like to sing from a prominent song post, but when the breeding season ends in July his singing will not be heard again, in full flow, until February comes around,

November 15

The grass is gradually disappearing under the rising flood waters. Unceasing rain has ensured that this part of the South West has been left shivering and submerged.
The local wildlife has made itself scarce in the face of such sodden weather.

November 16

Wet weather has meant that the water level has risen and small wavelets are lapping against the edge of the lake, Vegetation trails in the water providing cover for the wildlife.
Long hot days of summer now seem a long way off, as late autumn provides a glimpse of those winter months lying ahead.

November 17

There are flowers peeping through still, deep in the hedgerows where the colder weather has not made inroads.
The florets are bright against the late autumnal green surrounding leaves, and the brown leaves which have fallen from nearby trees and now carpet the ground.

November 18

A tufted duck bobs along in the middle of the lake, preferring the deeper water.
Such ducks breed in an area stretching from Iceland, across Russia to North America.
They can be seen in large lakes and bays.

.

November 19

Ferns are one of the oldest groups of plants in the world and many strains can grow with ease in differing soil types due to their ability to adapt. Depending on the climate they are growing in, they die back partially, or completely, this specimen by the lake having only partially died back so far.

November 20

It is unknown how many species of fungi there are growing in the natural world, but it has been claimed that if yeasts and molds are included then the number of different types could reach 50,000. The shades of fungi to be found vary from yellow, like this Par based example, through to pink.

November 21

A number of species of fungi are poisonous, of course, so the rule of thumb is just to leave those seen growing wild, such as this example sprouting in grass by the lake, well alone. It is said that DNA results reveal that a common ancestor of fungi was growing 600 million years ago.

November 22

The leaves have fallen from the trees, the evenings are now short and it is mostly evident that winter has arrived.
However, one sight is slightly out of synchronisation with other signs.
A new bud is spied, giving out the message that spring is waiting in the wings.

November 23

There has been flooding across the country today—especially in Cockermouth. Cockermouth may be a long way from Par, but here the heavens have opened as well, ensuring the level of the lake has risen quite starkly. This is highlighted by the fact that the 'Beware Deep Water' sign is gradually being obscured by water.

November 24

Two oystercatchers stand on the edge of the lake, keeping each other company. These sociable birds have long, orange bills which are designed to help them open shellfish such as cockles, and probe the earth for worms.
In their usual large flocks they are noisy, eye-catching birds.

November 25

Wind whips across the lake with real relish. The trees by the side of the lake, under which the ducks, swans and geese have gathered on hot days for shade, are now bending and swaying under the power of the gusts.

Today, the waterfowl are sheltering away from the weather elsewhere, mainly in the reeds.

November 26

Despite the wet, the wind and the falling temperatures, the gorse still continues to bloom although not, of course, in the same glorious fashion as during the months of May and June when the bushes across the dunes regularly flower in resplendent gold.

November 27

Raindrops continue to fall, dancing in droves on the surface of the stream which runs along the eastern side of the beach until it finally meets the sea.

Grasses, now brown and dry, bend under the onslaught of the rain and trail in the water. Kingfishers have been spotted in this area, their exceptionally eye-catching colours bright as they fly along the stream.

November 28

During the autumnal season the hedgerows, especially those around the lake, have been groaning with berries, and hips and haws.
Sloes have been taken by visitors for sloe gin while rosehips are often used, together with apples, to make rosehip syrup.

November 29

Amazingly, hidden away in the hedgerows, blackberry bushes are still in flower—although once the cold weather arrives in force that will quickly change.
The British blackberry season begins in June, reaches its peak in August and usually continues until the first frosts in November.

November 30

A full moon shines majestically over the lake.
Its rays illuminate the seagulls, clustering on the grass and flying in from the sea.
The reeds behind the island are also aglow, adding to the natural beauty on view.

December 1

December has arrived and thoughts are gradually turning to plans for Christmas Day. Gales, snow and plummeting temperatures are usually on the horizon at this time of year—but despite all the expected weather conditions—white florets of a thriving wild flower remain as bright as if it was still the height of summer.

December 2

It was the wettest November on record, a 'milestone' which is evident in, and around, the pond.
The area along the northern edge of the lake, which reaches one of the public footpaths, is awash.
The leafless trees are reflected in the water, now swirling across land which is usually just slightly boggy.

December 3

There are, definitely, regular inhabitants of the lake, such as the huge gaggle of Canada geese, that can be very noisy at times.
However, the numbers of wildfowl on the water are frequently swollen by new arrivals, who only stay for a couple of days, these geese an example of that phenomenon.

December 4

There is a hint of the tropics at the start of the last month of the year, as evident in one tree that could, perhaps, be growing on a beach in a warmer part of Europe.
The lake, with the houses of Polmear and the holiday park's chalets in the background, laps quite serenely.

December 5

Grasses, gorse and shrubs thrive in the dunes which divide the lake from long, sandy Par beach. They stand stark against a blue sky which looks anything but wintry on this particular December day.

December 6

Today, flooding has meant that the furthest reaches of the lake, that are usually only slightly muddy, or even dry, have become waterlogged almost overnight, as the ground was already so damp from November weather.
As a result, many of the ducks have been exploring differing areas of their territory.

December 7

A robin serenades the wildlife, and the evening visitors, to the lake.
Gone are the August days when the robins were quiet and their song could hardly be heard at all.
Now, as dusk falls, they are high in trees, marking their territory by letting the world know where they are, and that they are in charge—as this melodious character is doing

December 8

Dusk is falling and it is time to roost.
While some birds like to roost communally around the lake, as do the starlings in the reeds and the pied wagtails in the trees, not all of the local birds are so inclined.
Some of them are happier to roost in more solitary fashion.

December 9

The daisies and the dandelions are not at their most impressive in December, of course.
The dandelion's yellow flowers are best seen in the spring. The common dandelion has been used in medicinal systems around the globe for centuries, to improve digestion and treat ailments of the liver and spleen etc.

December 10

The swans are probably paying no attention to the weather, but a winter's fog, and slight rain, or Cornish mizzle, has swept across the lake, blocking the view to the island where a number of the ducks and geese maybe hiding away.
Occasionally, some of the swans take a short flight to the sea where they can be seen at the small river estuary at the west side of the beach.

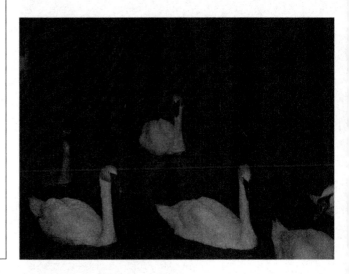

December 11

Daffodils traditionally bloom earlier than elsewhere in the country in Cornwall and the Isles of Scilly, and some are already peeping through near the lake.
These are near the trees along the footpath which leads from the beach entrance to the lake, and then onwards to the Mevagissey end of the sand, and of the holiday park.

December 12

The fog of a couple of days ago has disappeared and the swans are gathering once more in large numbers, but the ducks and geese are present among them on this occasion.
All seem to be enjoying a spell of December sun and blue skies, although the warmth of summer is obviously absent.

December 13

The reeds are reflected on the water as a pair of mallards swim peacefully by. The wind and rain have died down today which means the surface of the water is only slightly ruffled—rather than roughed up into wavelets as on some of the previous days.

December 14

It may be mid-December, but the natural area surrounding the lake is not just cloaked in differing shades of drab brown. Interspersed between vegetation which reflects the season are brighter, fresher colours—in this case light spring green.

December 15

Boulders frame the stream that runs from the lake to the east of the beach—and then out to sea. The cliff footpath, from here, will take walkers around the coast to the village of Polkerris and then to the port of Fowey from where a ferry runs to Polruan. The Saints' Way also runs through Par.

December 16

This cygnet still has its brown feathers, denoting its youth, but is proving its independence by swimming with the coots and the ducks, rather than with its parents.
The weather is cold and dry, with the odd shaft of winter sunshine.
The cygnet will definitely be leading a completely independent life soon

December 17

The time for picking blackberries this year to eat is now in the past, as revealed by these rather shrivelled, dried fruits.
Blackberry juice was sent to soldiers in the First World War after children were given days off school to go and pick as many as possible.

December 18

Frost has held nature in its grasp around the lake.
These grass blades are literally frozen. The frost will dissipate when the sun reaches this part of the pond's surroundings, and the air warms up.

December 19

The male blackbird, is all black with a yellow beak while the youngsters have mottled under-parts, along with upper-parts which are dark brown.
Nesting places are found in bushes and hedges, often in nearby gardens as well as around the lake itself.
Females will lay around four to five eggs between the months of April and June.
A pair of blackbirds have two to three broods.

December 20

The temperature has dropped overnight, and the geese and swans have woken up to discover that the lake has succumbed, in places, to ice, which means that some of them can walk on frozen water.
All seem unperturbed by the turn of events.

December 21

The ice has failed to melt completely, so although some of the waterfowl are swimming quite happily there are some who are still sliding around slightly because of the freezing conditions.
Most are congregating near the side of the pool, though, where the water runs free.

December 22

Oystercatchers gather in a small flock by the side of the lake.
The birds' winter plumage will not differ from their plumage throughout the year.
They commonly breed along the coasts of Britain. Their nests are just shallow depressions in which they usually have three eggs in May.

December 23

A Song thrush search-es for worms and other insects in the grass.
Resident birds, Song thrushes breed throughout the British Isles, although some living in the north move south in the winter when visitors arrive from the Continent.

December 24

A robin is camouflaged by the reeds he is perched in, and can hardly be seen.
Christmas Eve is relatively mild compared to some of the weather so today the pond is free of ice and no rain has fallen from the Cornish skies.
The robin is only small, growing to 14 cm, so can quite easily hide in the undergrowth.

December 25

Christmas Day, and sunset illuminates a calm sea on Par beach. To the west lies Black Head and a number of beaches between Par and the fishing port of Mevagissey—these beaches and villages including Duporth, or black cove in Cornish, Charlestown, Porthpean and Pentewan.

December 26

Dropping temperatures have led to ice forming on the lake. The residents have mostly absented themselves from view, and are hiding in the reeds, and in the island which cannot be easily reached by humans and, as a result, is territory that is almost always inhabited by birds and animals only.
The ice is only thin, however, and can already be seen to be thawing in places'

December 27

There have been a few hours of misty rain during the day, sweeping across Par beach and the lake. Often there are shags and cormorants on view on the rocks that can be found to the west of the beach. However, there are none on view today due to an absence of dry weather and sun of any kind.

December 28

There are blue skies for this late December day, and in the fine, clear weather two jackdaws perch in one of the trees by the lake.

The birds enjoy socialising and tend to nest together in the holes of trees, walls and rocks.

It is thought that some jackdaws migrate to Britain during winter months.

December 29

A cold, grey, misty day as the year edges to a close. A few hardy souls take a walk on Par Beach while the ducks on the lake, lapping on the other side of the sand dunes, are mainly settling down on the island on the north side of the pool.

To the east lies Gribbin Head while to the west, between Par and Mevagissey lies Black Head and the villages of Charlestown and Pentewan.

December 30

People returning from the beach at Par to one of the car parks are able to spy the lake through the trees. Linking the pool with the beach are a number of sandy footpaths that run through the dunes, which seem to expand further seawards each year.

Those returning to the car park can spy the seagulls and waterfowl gathering on the edge of the lake.

December 31

There is a flurry of gulls' wings over the lake on the last day of the year, with the holiday park caravans serving as the background to such activity— although later these are to be replaced by chalets and mobile homes.
The pond at Par Beach, which is home to so much wildlife, has been in place for well over 100 years and was once known as the Model Yacht Pond.
It is a favourite gathering place for the gulls, who also have Par Bay itself as a source for food.
Through the years fish caught in the Bay have ranged from mackerel to mullet and skate to bass and pilchards.
Around the cliffs, at Polkerris, there was a 'fish palace' where the fish from the local fishing boats was processed, and then packed. Parts of the building can still be spied at the back of the Polkerris beach.

Printed in Great Britain
by Amazon

18967981R00078